A
MEDITATIVE
COMMENTARY
ON THE
NEW TESTAMENT

JOHN: BELIEVING IN JESUS

By Gary Holloway

LEAFWOOD
PUBLISHERS

JOHN: BELIEVING IN JESUS
Published by Leafwood Publishers

Copyright 2007 by Gary Holloway

ISBN 978-0-89112-504-4
Printed in the United States of America

Cover design by Greg Jackson, Jackson Design Co., llc

For information contact:
Leafwood Publishers, Abilene, Texas
1-877-816-4455 toll free
www.leafwoodpublishers.com

07 08 09 10 11 12 / 7 6 5 4 3 2 1

To John York, faithful friend

C O N T E N T S

INTRODUCTION

MEDITATIONS

INTRODUCTION

HEARING GOD IN SCRIPTURE

Many good commentaries, guides, and workbooks exist on the various books of the Bible. How is this series different? It is not intended to answer all your scholarly questions about the Bible, or even make you an expert in the details of Scripture. Instead, this series is designed to help you hear the voice of God for your everyday life. It is a guide to meditation on the Bible, meditation that will allow the Bible to transform you.

We read in many ways. We might scan the newspaper for information, read a map for location, read a novel for pleasure, or read a textbook to pass a test. These are all good ways to read, depending on our circumstances.

A young soldier far away from home who receives a letter from his wife reads in yet another way. He might scan the letter quickly at first for news and information. But his longing for his beloved causes him to read the letter again and again, hearing her sweet voice in every line. He slowly treasures each word of this precious letter.

BIBLE STUDY

So also, there are many good ways to read the Bible, depending on our circumstances. Bible study is absolutely necessary for our life with God. We rightly study the Bible for information. We ask, "Who wrote this?" "When was it written?" "Who were the original readers?"

"How do these words apply to me?" More importantly, we want information about God. Who is he? What does he think of me? What does he want from me?

There is no substitute for this kind of close, dedicated Bible study. We must know what the Bible says to know our standing with God. We therefore read the Bible to discover true doctrine or teaching. But some in their emphasis on the authority and inspiration of the Bible have forgotten that Bible study is not an end in itself. We want to know God through Scripture. We want to have a relationship with the Teacher, not just the teachings.

Jesus tells some of God's people in his day, "You diligently study the Scriptures because you think that by them you possess eternal life. These are the Scriptures that testify about me, yet you refuse to come to me to have life" (John 5:39-40). He's not telling them to study their Bibles less, but he is reminding them of the deeper purpose of Bible study—to draw us to God through Jesus. Bible study is a means, not an end.

Yet the way many of us have learned to study the Bible may actually get in the way of hearing God. "Bible study" may sound a lot like schoolwork, and many of us were happy to get out of school. "Bible study" may call to mind pictures of intellectuals surrounded by books in Greek and Hebrew, pondering meanings too deep for ordinary people. The method of Bible study that has been popular for some time focuses on the strangeness of the Bible. It was written long ago, far away, and in languages we cannot read. There is a huge gap between us and the original readers of the Bible, a gap that can only be bridged by scholars, not by average folk.

There is some truth and some value in that "scholarly" method. It is true that the Bible was not written originally to us. Knowing ancient languages and customs can at times help us understand the Bible better. However, one unintended result of this approach is to make the Bible distant from the people of God. We may come to think that we can only hear God indirectly through Scripture, that his word must be filtered through scholars. We may even think that deep Bible study is a matter of mastering obscure information about the Bible.

MEDITATION

But we read the Bible for more than information. By studying it, we experience transformation, the mysterious process of God at work in us. Through his loving words, God is calling us to life with him. He is forming us into the image of his Son.

Reading the Bible is not like reading other books. We are not simply trying to learn information or master material. Instead, we want to stand under the authority of Scripture and let God master us. While we read the Bible, it reads us, opening the depths of our being to the overpowering love of God. "For the word of God is living and active. Sharper than any double-edged sword, it penetrates even to dividing soul and spirit, joints and marrow; it judges the thoughts and attitudes of the heart. Nothing in all creation is hidden from God's sight. Everything is uncovered and laid bare before the eyes of him to whom we must give account" (Hebrews 4:12-13).

Opening our hearts to the word of God is meditation. Although this way of reading the Bible may be new to some, it has a long heritage among God's people. The Psalmist joyously meditates on the words of God (Psalm 1:2; 39:3; 119:15, 23, 27, 48, 78, 97, 99, 148). Meditation is taking the words of Scripture to heart and letting them ask questions of us. It is slowing chewing over a text, listening closely, reading God's message of love to us over and over. This is not a simple, easy, or naïve reading of Scripture, but a process that takes time, dedication, and practice on our part.

There are many ways to meditate on the Bible. One is praying the Scriptures. Prayer and Bible study really cannot be separated. One way of praying the Bible is to make the words of a text your prayer. Obviously, the prayer texts of Scripture, especially the Psalms, lend themselves to this. "The Lord is my shepherd" has been the prayer of many hearts.

However, it is proper and helpful to turn the words of the Bible into prayers. Commands from God can become prayers. "You shall have no other gods before me" (Exodus 20:3) can be prayed, "Lord, keep me from anything that takes your place in my heart." Stories can be prayed. Jesus heals a man born blind (John 9), and so we pray, "Lord Jesus open my eyes to who you truly are." Even the promises of the Bible become prayers. "Never will I leave you; never will I forsake you" (Deuteronomy 31:6; Hebrews 13:5) becomes "God help me know that you promise that you are always with me and so live my life without fear."

Obviously, there are many helpful ways of hearing the voice of God in Scripture. Again, the purpose of Bible reading and study is not to know more about the Bible, much less to pride ourselves as experts on Scripture. Instead, we read to hear the voice of our Beloved. We listen for a word of God for us.

Holy Reading

This commentary reflects one ancient way of meditation and praying the Scriptures known as lectio divina or holy reading. This method assumes that God wants to speak to us directly in the Bible, that the passage we are reading is God's word to us right now. The writers of the New Testament read the Old Testament with this same conviction. They saw the words of the Bible speaking directly to their own situation. They read with humility and with prayer.

The first step along this way of holy reading is listening to the Bible. Choose a biblical text that is not too long. This commentary breaks the

Gospel of John into smaller sections. The purpose is to hear God's voice in your current situation, not to cover material or prepare lessons. Get into a comfortable position and maintain silence before God for several minutes. This prepares the heart to listen. Read slowly. Savor each word. Perhaps read aloud. Listen for a particular phrase that speaks to you. Ask God, "What are you trying to tell me today?"

The next step is to meditate on that particular phrase. That meditation may include slowly repeating the phrase that seems to be for you today. As you think deeply on it, you might even memorize it. Committing biblical passages to memory allows us to hold them in our hearts all day long. If you keep a journal, you might write the passage there. Let those words sink deeply into your heart.

Then pray those words back to God in your heart. Those words may call up visual images, smells, sounds, and feelings. Pay attention to what God is giving you in those words. Then respond in faith to what those words say to your heart. What do they call you to be and to do? Our humble response might take the form of praise, thanksgiving, joy, confession, or even cries of pain.

The final step in this "holy reading" is contemplation of God. The words from God that we receive deeply in our hearts lead us to him. Through these words, we experience union with the all-powerful God of love. Again, one should not separate Bible reading from prayer. The words of God in Scripture transport us into the very presence of God where we joyfully rest in his love.

What keeps reading the Bible this way from becoming merely our own desires read back into Scripture? How do we know it is God's voice we hear and not our own?

Two things. One is prayer. We are asking God to open our hearts, minds, and lives to him. We ask to hear his voice, not ours and not the voice of the world around us.

The second thing that keeps this from being an exercise in self-deception is to study the Bible in community. By praying over

Scripture in a group, we hear God's word together. God speaks through the other members of our group. The wisdom he gives them keeps us from private, selfish, and unusual interpretations. They help us keep our own voices in check, as we desire to listen to God alone.

HOW TO USE THIS COMMENTARY

This commentary provides assistance in holy reading of the Bible. It gives structure to daily personal devotions, family meditation, small group Bible studies, and church classes.

DAILY DEVOTIONAL

Listening, meditation, prayer, contemplation. How does this commentary fit into this way of Bible study? Consider it as a conversation partner. We have taken a section of Scripture and then broken it down into four short daily readings. After listening, meditating, praying, and contemplating the passage for the day, use the questions suggested in the commentary to provoke deeper reflection. This provides a structure for a daily fifteen minute devotional four days a week. On the fifth day, read the entire passage, meditate, and then use the questions to reflect on the meaning of the whole. On day six, take our meditations on the passage as conversation with another who has prayed over the text.

If you want to begin daily Bible reading, but need guidance, this provides a Monday-Saturday experience that prepares the heart for worship and praise on Sunday. This structure also results in a communal reading of Scripture, instead of a private reading. Even if you use this commentary alone, you are not reading privately. God is at work in you and in the conversation you have with another (the author of the commentary) who has sought to hear God through this passage of the Bible.

FAMILY BIBLE STUDY

This commentary can also provide an arrangement for family Bible study. Many Christian parents want to lead their children in daily study, but don't know where to begin or how to structure their time. Using the six-day plan outlined above means the entire family can read, meditate, pray, and reflect on the shorter passages, using the questions provided. On day five, they can review the entire passage, and then on day six, read the meditations in the commentary to prompt reflection and discussion. God will bless our families beyond our imaginations through the prayerful study of his word.

WEEKLY GROUP STUDY

This commentary can also structure small group Bible study. Each member of the group should have meditated over the daily readings and questions for the five days preceding the group meeting, using the method outlined above. The day before the group meeting, each member should read and reflect on the meditations in the commentary on that passage. You then can meet once a week to hear God's word together. In that group meeting, the method of holy reading would look something like this:

Listening
1. Five minutes of silence.
2. Slow reading of the biblical passage for that week.

3. A minute of silent meditation on the passage.

4. Briefly share with the group the word or phrase that struck you.

Personal Message

5. A second reading of the same passage.

6. A minute of silence.

7. Where does this touch your life today?

8. Responses: I hear, I see, etc.

Life Response

9. Brief silence.

10. What does God want you to do today in light of this word?

Group Prayer

11. Have each member of the group pray aloud for the person on his or her left, asking God to bless the word he has given them.

The procedure suggested here can be used in churches or in neighborhood Bible studies. Church members would use the daily readings Monday-Friday in their daily devotionals. This commentary intentionally provides no readings on the sixth day, so that we can spend Saturdays as a time of rest, not rest from Bible study, but a time to let God's word quietly work its way deep into our hearts. Sunday during Bible school or in home meetings, the group would meet to experience the weekly readings together, using the group method described above. It might be that the sermon for each Sunday could be on the passage for that week.

Some churches have used this structure to great advantage. In the hallways of those church buildings, the talk is not of the local football team or the weather, but of the shared experience of the Word of God for that week.

And that is the purpose of our personal and communal study, to hear the voice of God, our loving Father who wants us to love him in return. He deeply desires a personal relationship with us. Father, Son, and Spirit make a home inside us (see John 14:16-17, 23). Our loving God speaks to his children! But we must listen for his voice. That listening is not a matter of gritting our teeth and trying harder to hear. Instead, it is part of our entire life with God. That is what Bible study is all about.

Through daily personal prayer and meditation on God's word and through a communal reading of Scripture, our most important conversation partner, the Holy Spirit, will do his mysterious and marvelous work. Among other things, the Spirit pours God's love into our hearts (Romans 5:5), bears witness to our spirits that we are God's children (Romans 8:16), intercedes for us with God (Romans 8:26), and enlightens us as to God's will (Ephesians 1:17).

So this is an invitation to personal daily Bible study, to praying the Scriptures, to sharing with fellow believers, to hear the voice of God. God will bless us, our families, our churches, and his world if we take the time to be still, listen, and do his word.

THE SPIRITUALITY OF JOHN

Written by one who calls himself "the disciple whom Jesus loved," the Gospel of John paints an intimate portrait of Jesus. The Gospel portrays Jesus as one who is intimate with God the Father, who calls disciples to follow him, and who gives signs that point his listeners to God. In John, Jesus tells us precisely who he is. "I am the bread of life" (John 6:35). "I am the light of the world" (John 8:12). "I am the door of the sheep" (John 10:7). "I am the good shepherd" (John 10:11). "I am the resurrection, and the life" (John 11:25). "I am the way, the truth, and the life" (John 14:6). "I am the true vine" (John 15:1).

Most importantly, Jesus says, "I am in my Father, and you are in me, and I am in you" (John 14:20). This dynamic identification with the Father and with us is through the Holy Spirit. More than any other gospel, John focuses on the Spirit as the vehicle of God's presence in Jesus and in us. John is foremost a spiritual gospel.

THE SPIRIT IN JESUS

John the Baptist testifies that the Spirit came down upon Jesus at his baptism and remained on him (John 1:32-33). It is the Holy Spirit who empowers Jesus for ministry, allowing him to work amazing signs that point to his identity as the Messiah. Jesus has the Spirit without limit, so he speaks the words of God (John 3:34).

JESUS GIVES THE SPIRIT

Spirituality in the Gospel of John is the actual experience of the Holy Spirit. Again, John the Baptist says, "I would not have known him, except that the one who sent me to baptize with water told me, 'The man on whom you see the Spirit come down and remain is he who will baptize with the Holy Spirit'" (John 1:33). The followers of Jesus are not only baptized with water, but are immersed in the Holy Spirit. After his resurrection, Jesus breathes on the disciples and says, "Receive the Holy Spirit" (John 20:22). The Father sends the Spirit on the Son who in turn shares the Holy Spirit with his disciples, giving them power and guidance for ministry.

THE SPIRIT OF LIFE

It is the Holy Spirit who gives life to believers, pointing them to the one who is Life, that is, Jesus. Jesus describes this new and fuller life in the Spirit as being born anew (or from above) by water and the Spirit (John 3:3-8). Nicodemus does not understand what Jesus is saying, but later Jesus clearly says, "The Spirit gives life; the flesh counts for nothing. The words I have spoken to you are spirit and they are life" (John 6:63). The new and abundant life Jesus promises comes only through the Holy Spirit. Genuine Christian spirituality is life-affirming and life-giving.

THE SPIRIT OF TRUTH

The gospel of John is full of testimony. John the Baptist, Andrew, Philip, the Samaritan woman, Mary Magdalene, and many others testify to the identity of Jesus. Jesus himself, the words he speaks, and the signs he performs all are true testimony. Indeed, the whole purpose of the Gospel of John is to give testimony so that those who have never seen Jesus might still believe that he is the Christ, the Son of God (John 20:31).

However, more than human witnesses point to Jesus. The Holy Spirit also bears witness. He is the Spirit of truth, who guides disciples into all truth (John 16:13). If one wants to be a disciple one must follow Jesus. Only then will the Spirit guide the true disciple into the truth that gives freedom (John 8:31-32).

THE SPIRIT AS THE PRESENCE OF JESUS

When Jesus talks of leaving the disciples, they are understandably shaken. How can they have life without the presence of Jesus? However Jesus says it is actually better for them that he is going, so he can send the Counselor, the Holy Spirit to them (see John 16:1-16). In this word—translated Counselor, Helper, Comforter, and Advocate— we experience the heart of the spirituality of John's gospel. The Spirit is the ongoing presence of Christ. The Jesus who was with the original disciples in a physical body now lives in the bodies of disciples through the Holy Spirit. At its center, Christian spirituality is not about techniques, pious feelings, or heroic actions but is the actual presence and work of the Father and the Son in our lives through the Holy Spirit.

To summarize, in the Gospel of John spirituality is the presence of God the Father, given to Jesus without limit. Jesus in turn gives the Spirit to disciples as his presence in them. That presence in the disciples gives life and truth, overflowing in blessings to others (John 7:38-39).

MEDITATIONS

WORD AND LIGHT

(John 1:1-34)

Day One Reading and Questions:

¹In the beginning was the Word, and the Word was with God, and the Word was God. ²He was with God in the beginning.

³Through him all things were made; without him nothing was made that has been made. ⁴In him was life, and that life was the light of men. ⁵The light shines in the darkness, but the darkness has not understood it.

1. How is Jesus like a word? What do words do? What does Jesus do?

2. How does Jesus give life? How is this more than mere existence?

3. What does light do? How is Jesus like light?

Day Two Reading and Questions:

⁶There came a man who was sent from God; his name was John. ⁷He came as a witness to testify concerning that light, so that through

him all men might believe. [8]He himself was not the light; he came only as a witness to the light. [9]The true light that gives light to every man was coming into the world.

[10]He was in the world, and though the world was made through him, the world did not recognize him. [11]He came to that which was his own, but his own did not receive him. [12]Yet to all who received him, to those who believed in his name, he gave the right to become children of God—[13]children born not of natural descent, nor of human decision or a husband's will, but born of God.

[14]The Word became flesh and made his dwelling among us. We have seen his glory, the glory of the One and Only, who came from the Father, full of grace and truth.

1. What was the role of John the Baptist? Why was his work necessary?

2. What does it mean to be a child of God? How do we become children of God? What is the relationship between Jesus as God's Son and us as God's children?

3. How does Jesus reveal God? What kind of God do we see in Jesus?

DAY THREE READING AND QUESTIONS:

[15]John testifies concerning him. He cries out, saying, "This was he of whom I said, 'He who comes after me has surpassed me because he was before me.'" [16]From the fullness of his grace we have all received one blessing after another. [17]For the law was given through Moses; grace and truth came through Jesus Christ. [18]No one has ever seen God, but God the One and Only, who is at the Father's side, has made him known.

¹⁹Now this was John's testimony when the Jews of Jerusalem sent priests and Levites to ask him who he was. ²⁰He did not fail to confess, but confessed freely, "I am not the Christ."

²¹They asked him, "Then who are you? Are you Elijah?"

He said, "I am not."

"Are you the Prophet?"

He answered, "No."

²²Finally they said, "Who are you? Give us an answer to take back to those who sent us. What do you say about yourself?"

²³John replied in the words of Isaiah the prophet, "I am the voice of one calling in the desert, 'Make straight the way for the Lord.'"

²⁴Now some Pharisees who had been sent ²⁵questioned him, "Why then do you baptize if you are not the Christ, nor Elijah, nor the Prophet?"

²⁶"I baptize with water," John replied, "but among you stands one you do not know. ²⁷He is the one who comes after me, the thongs of whose sandals I am not worthy to untie."

²⁸This all happened at Bethany on the other side of the Jordan, where John was baptizing.

1. *Why is testimony important? What was John's testimony regarding Jesus?*

2. *How does John describe himself? How does that description relate to Jesus as the Word?*

3. *Why was John's baptizing important?*

DAY FOUR READING AND QUESTIONS:

²⁹The next day John saw Jesus coming toward him and said, "Look, the Lamb of God, who takes away the sin of the world! ³⁰This

is the one I meant when I said, 'A man who comes after me has surpassed me because he was before me.' [31]I myself did not know him, but the reason I came baptizing with water was that he might be revealed to Israel."

[32]Then John gave this testimony: "I saw the Spirit come down from heaven as a dove and remain on him. [33]I would not have known him, except that the one who sent me to baptize with water told me, 'The man on whom you see the Spirit come down and remain is he who will baptize with the Holy Spirit.' [34]I have seen and I testify that this is the Son of God."

1. *What is the significance of the Lamb of God? What were lambs used for in Israel?*

2. *When does the Spirit remain on Jesus? Why is this important to those who have been baptized into Jesus?*

3. *Why is the Spirit associated with a dove? What does this tell us about the nature of the Spirit?*

DAY FIVE READING AND QUESTIONS:

Go back and read the entire passage.

1. *Why is it important that we have witnesses about Jesus? How are we to be witnesses?*

2. *Why did the darkness not understand the light? Why does the world not recognize Jesus? If Jesus reveals God, what keeps some from seeing him?*

3. How does one receive or accept the testimony about Jesus?

MEDITATION ON JOHN 1:1-34

Imagine being trapped alone in a dark mine, able to do nothing but wait in darkness and silence for your rescuers.

A word. For a person alone, a word is precious. They long for a word.

Light. For one trapped in darkness, there is nothing more precious. Just a glimpse of light is salvation.

Jesus comes as Word and Light. A Word from God. How precious that is. How much we take it for granted. But what if there were no word from God? What if we were alone in the universe, straining to hear a word about the meaning of our lives but hearing nothing? Then we would long for a word. What if we were trapped in a mine? Straining to hear our rescuers, desperate for a light in the darkness. How precious that light would be.

Jesus comes as Word and Light. Not a word shouted over the distance or a light from a far-away star. He comes close. He becomes one of us. The Word near. The Light within.

But will we hear that Word and embrace that Light? Will we receive him, believe in him, and accept him? Can we trust his gifts—grace and truth and glory and Spirit? How much do we long for Word and Light?

That's the question the Gospel of John asks. We must answer not just in words but with our lives.

"Jesus, Word of God made flesh, open our hearts to receive you in faith. Open our eyes to see your Light."

TESTIMONY AND DISCIPLES

(John 1:35-2:12)

Day One Reading and Questions:

35The next day John was there again with two of his disciples.
36When he saw Jesus passing by, he said, "Look, the Lamb of God!"
37When the two disciples heard him say this, they followed Jesus.
38Turning around, Jesus saw them following and asked, "What do you want?"

They said, "Rabbi" (which means Teacher), "where are you staying?"

39"Come," he replied, "and you will see."

So they went and saw where he was staying, and spent that day with him. It was about the tenth hour.
40Andrew, Simon Peter's brother, was one of the two who heard what John had said and who had followed Jesus. 41The first thing Andrew did was to find his brother Simon and tell him, "We have found the Messiah" (that is, the Christ). 42And he brought him to Jesus.

Jesus looked at him and said, "You are Simon son of John. You will be called Cephas" (which, when translated, is Peter).

1. Why is it important that Jesus is called "Rabbi" or teacher?

2. "Come and see." Is this more than an invitation from Jesus to see where he is staying? Is this invitation for us today?

3. Why does Jesus change Simon's name? Who else in the Bible had their name changed? What does a name change signify?

DAY TWO READING AND QUESTIONS:

[43]The next day Jesus decided to leave for Galilee. Finding Philip, he said to him, "Follow me."

[44]Philip, like Andrew and Peter, was from the town of Bethsaida. [45]Philip found Nathanael and told him, "We have found the one Moses wrote about in the Law, and about whom the prophets also wrote—Jesus of Nazareth, the son of Joseph."

[46]"Nazareth! Can anything good come from there?" Nathanael asked.

"Come and see," said Philip.

[47]When Jesus saw Nathanael approaching, he said of him, "Here is a true Israelite, in whom there is nothing false."

[48]"How do you know me?" Nathanael asked.

Jesus answered, "I saw you while you were still under the fig tree before Philip called you."

[49]Then Nathanael declared, "Rabbi, you are the Son of God; you are the King of Israel."

[50]Jesus said, "You believe because I told you I saw you under the fig tree. You shall see greater things than that." [51]He then added, "I tell you the truth, you shall see heaven open, and the angels of God ascending and descending on the Son of Man."

1. What was the first thing Philip did after Jesus called him to follow? Why?

2. Nathaniel looked down on Jesus because he was from Nazareth. Do we sometimes put down others because of their hometown? Did Nathaniel completely dismiss Jesus?

3. Why does Nathaniel react so strongly to Jesus, calling him the Son of God and the King of Israel? Does this have anything to do with testimony and witnessing?

Day Three Reading and Questions:

¹On the third day a wedding took place at Cana in Galilee. Jesus' mother was there, ²and Jesus and his disciples had also been invited to the wedding. ³When the wine was gone, Jesus' mother said to him, "They have no more wine."

⁴"Dear woman, why do you involve me?" Jesus replied, "My time has not yet come."

⁵His mother said to the servants, "Do whatever he tells you."

⁶Nearby stood six stone water jars, the kind used by the Jews for ceremonial washing, each holding from twenty to thirty gallons.

1. Why did Mary tell Jesus about the wine? What do you think she expected him to do? Had Mary seen Jesus perform miracles before this?

2. What does Jesus mean by "My time has not yet come?"

3. Is it significant that all this takes place at a wedding? How is a wedding used elsewhere in the Bible to talk about our relationship with God?

Day Four Reading and Questions:

[7]Jesus said to the servants, "Fill the jars with water"; so they filled them to the brim.

[8]Then he told them, "Now draw some out and take it to the master of the banquet."

They did so, [9]and the master of the banquet tasted the water that had been turned into wine. He did not realize where it had come from, though the servants who had drawn the water knew. Then he called the bridegroom aside [10]and said, "Everyone brings out the choice wine first and then the cheaper wine after the guests have had too much to drink; but you have saved the best till now."

[11]This, the first of his miraculous signs, Jesus performed in Cana of Galilee. He thus revealed his glory, and his disciples put their faith in him.

[12]After this he went down to Capernaum with his mother and brothers and his disciples. There they stayed for a few days.

1. *Why did Jesus tell his mother, "My time has not yet come" and then go ahead and turn the water to wine? Was it his time or not?*

2. *The master of the banquet says, "You have saved the best until now." Can this statement apply to more than wine?*

3. *Why is this act called a "sign"? To what does it point?*

Day Five Reading and Questions:

Go back and read the entire passage.

1. *List all the people who testify or bear witness to Jesus in these verses.*

2. *What do those people say about Jesus?*

3. *What are the results of their testimony?*

MEDITATION ON JOHN 1:35-2:12

Who do you believe? Who do you follow?

Perhaps (like me) you tend to be cynical and believe little and follow no one. We have believed before and been burned. We have followed and been disappointed.

We are a lot like Nathaniel. His friend Philip tells him, "We have found the one we have been waiting for." Nathaniel finds that hard to believe, especially since Jesus comes from Nazareth. Surely the one we've been waiting for will come from somewhere better than that!

But Nathaniel is willing to do what Philip asks, "Come and see." He goes and sees Jesus for himself. Sees. Hears. Believes. Follows.

Are we willing to do the same? Of course we are! We've known Jesus all our lives! We believe in him! We follow him!

Do we? Are we willing to follow when we see where he stays? He has no permanent, comfortable home. Are we willing to follow him when he knows where we have been, he knows us inside out? Are we willing to be known that much? Are we willing, like the servants in the story, to do what he says when it makes no sense? To fill pots with water, take it to the master of the feast, and claim it is wine? Are we willing to believe water can be wine? Are we willing to join a Jesus who makes gallons of wine when we might get kicked out of our church for bringing a bottle to a reception?

Are we willing to follow the Lamb of God, knowing that he goes to the slaughter?

It's easy to dismiss the testimony about Jesus, "We have found the Messiah." It's even easier to convince ourselves we believe and follow, when we are not willing to go with him wherever he goes.

"Lord Jesus, we believe, help our unbelief. We follow, but only in part. Make us your disciples. Open our eyes. Change our hearts."

NEW TEMPLE, NEW BIRTH

(John 2:13-3:21)

DAY ONE READING AND QUESTIONS:

¹³When it was almost time for the Jewish Passover, Jesus went up to Jerusalem. ¹⁴In the temple courts he found men selling cattle, sheep and doves, and others sitting at tables exchanging money. ¹⁵So he made a whip out of cords, and drove all from the temple area, both sheep and cattle; he scattered the coins of the money changers and overturned their tables. ¹⁶To those who sold doves he said, "Get these out of here! How dare you turn my Father's house into a market!"

1. Jesus seems angry and violent here. Is this our usual picture of Jesus? Why not?

2. Why did Jesus drive out the sellers and the moneychangers?

3. Do we today sometimes turn God's house, the church, into a market? How?

Day Two Reading and Questions:

[17]His disciples remembered that it is written: "Zeal for your house will consume me."

[18]Then the Jews demanded of him, "What miraculous sign can you show us to prove your authority to do all this?"

[19]Jesus answered them, "Destroy this temple, and I will raise it again in three days."

[20]The Jews replied, "It has taken forty-six years to build this temple, and you are going to raise it in three days?" [21]But the temple he had spoken of was his body. [22]After he was raised from the dead, his disciples recalled what he had said. Then they believed the Scripture and the words that Jesus had spoken.

1. *How does this act show Jesus' passion or zeal for God's house? How do we show our passion for God?*

2. *Why was it so shocking that Jesus promised to destroy the temple?*

3. *Can one build up others without tearing down evil? Is there a destructive side to the mission of Jesus?*

Day Three Reading and Questions:

[23]Now while he was in Jerusalem at the Passover Feast, many people saw the miraculous signs he was doing and believed in his name. [24]But Jesus would not entrust himself to them, for he knew all men. [25]He did not need man's testimony about man, for he knew what was in a man.

[1]Now there was a man of the Pharisees named Nicodemus, a member of the Jewish ruling council. [2]He came to Jesus at night and

said, "Rabbi, we know you are a teacher who has come from God. For no one could perform the miraculous signs you are doing if God were not with him."

³In reply Jesus declared, "I tell you the truth, no one can see the kingdom of God unless he is born again."

⁴"How can a man be born when he is old?" Nicodemus asked. "Surely he cannot enter a second time into his mother's womb to be born!"

⁵Jesus answered, "I tell you the truth, no one can enter the kingdom of God unless he is born of water and the Spirit. ⁶Flesh gives birth to flesh, but the Spirit gives birth to spirit. ⁷You should not be surprised at my saying, 'You must be born again.' ⁸The wind blows wherever it pleases. You hear its sound, but you cannot tell where it comes from or where it is going. So it is with everyone born of the Spirit."

1. *What does it mean that Jesus would not entrust himself to some who believed? Did he entrust himself to Nicodemus?*

2. *Why does Nicodemus find the idea of being born again so shocking?*

3. *What exactly is spiritual birth? How is it similar to physical birth? How is it different?*

Day Four Reading and Questions:

⁹"How can this be?" Nicodemus asked.

¹⁰"You are Israel's teacher," said Jesus, "and do you not understand these things? ¹¹I tell you the truth, we speak of what we know, and we testify to what we have seen, but still you people do not accept our testimony. ¹²I have spoken to you of earthly things and you do not believe; how then will you believe if I speak of heavenly things? ¹³No one has ever gone into heaven except the one who came from

heaven—the Son of Man. [14]Just as Moses lifted up the snake in the desert, so the Son of Man must be lifted up, [15]that everyone who believes in him may have eternal life.

[16]"For God so loved the world that he gave his one and only Son, that whoever believes in him shall not perish but have eternal life. [17]For God did not send his Son into the world to condemn the world, but to save the world through him. [18]Whoever believes in him is not condemned, but whoever does not believe stands condemned already because he has not believed in the name of God's one and only Son. [19]This is the verdict: Light has come into the world, but men loved darkness instead of light because their deeds were evil. [20]Everyone who does evil hates the light, and will not come into the light for fear that his deeds will be exposed. [21]But whoever lives by the truth comes into the light, so that it may be seen plainly that what he has done has been done through God."

1. *What is the testimony of Jesus? What does he speak about? How does one accept his testimony?*

2. *Why did God send his Son? Why do some still think Jesus came to condemn the world? Do you know Christians who think this?*

3. *Why would anyone reject the light?*

Day Five Reading and Questions:

Go back and read the entire passage.

1. *What connection can you see between clearing the temple and telling Nicodemus he must be born again?*

2. *What if you were told to give up everything you have, believe, and know in order to start all over again? Could you do it? Are we ready for such a radical change?*

3. *What are some ways that Christians have gotten in the way of God's love for the world?*

MEDITATION ON JOHN 2:13-3:21

I remember playing a board game as a kid. I can't remember what it was but the object was to roll the dice, move certain spaces, and be the first to arrive at the finish. I was ahead of everyone, only a few spaces from the finish line when I announced, "Nothing can stop me now." So I rolled the dice, moved the correct number of spaces, and landed on the most dreaded space of all—the one that said, "Return to Start."

That must be the way Nicodemus felt. He was a ruler of the people. He had some experience and wisdom. He had served God all his life. Now he comes to this new Rabbi, Jesus, who tells him he has to return to the very start. He has to be born all over.

Nicodemus can't believe it. "How can a man be born when he is old?" I don't think Nicodemus is so thick that he takes Jesus literally. I think he took him seriously. Having lived enough to learn how to live, he now must give it all up and start over. No wonder he asks, "How can this be?"

Nicodemus was not alone. His fellow believers had spent years building the temple. They dreamed of the splendor of that building that would give glory to God. True, some didn't understand the purpose of the temple. They had turned it into a market. But some did understand that it was built to give glory to God. Now here comes this Jesus who speaks of destroying the temple, then rebuilding it in three days! No wonder they didn't understand. God no longer would live in a building but in a body.

Nicodemus and those at the temple are not alone. We also struggle with Jesus if we take him seriously. He embodies God's love for the whole world. Not just the good people, the respectable people, the religious people. The whole world. For those of us who have spent a lifetime being religious and building temples for God, he has a clear message.

Return to start.

"God of love, you love the whole world. May we give up our knowledge, our religion, and the kingdoms we build. May we love and not condemn."

WATER AND FOOD

(John 3:22-4:42)

DAY ONE READING AND QUESTIONS:

²²After this, Jesus and his disciples went out into the Judean countryside, where he spent some time with them, and baptized. ²³Now John also was baptizing at Aenon near Salim, because there was plenty of water, and people were constantly coming to be baptized. ²⁴(This was before John was put in prison.) ²⁵An argument developed between some of John's disciples and a certain Jew over the matter of ceremonial washing. ²⁶They came to John and said to him, "Rabbi, that man who was with you on the other side of the Jordan—the one you testified about—well, he is baptizing, and everyone is going to him."

²⁷To this John replied, "A man can receive only what is given him from heaven. ²⁸You yourselves can testify that I said, 'I am not the Christ but am sent ahead of him.' ²⁹The bride belongs to the bridegroom. The friend who attends the bridegroom waits and listens for him, and is full of joy when he hears the bridegroom's voice. That joy is mine, and it is now complete. ³⁰He must become greater; I must become less.

³¹"The one who comes from above is above all; the one who is from the earth belongs to the earth, and speaks as one from the earth. The one who comes from heaven is above all. ³²He testifies to what

he has seen and heard, but no one accepts his testimony. [33]The man who has accepted it has certified that God is truthful. [34]For the one whom God has sent speaks the words of God, for God gives the Spirit without limit. [35]The Father loves the Son and has placed everything in his hands. [36]Whoever believes in the Son has eternal life, but whoever rejects the Son will not see life, for God's wrath remains on him."

1. How hard do you think it was for John to see everyone abandoning him for Jesus? Is it easy to say, "He must become greater; I must become less"?

2. John says no one accepts the testimony of the one from heaven. Is this true or an exaggeration? Did no one accept the testimony of Jesus?

3. God gives Jesus the Spirit without limit. Is our experience of the Spirit the same as that of Jesus?

DAY TWO READING AND QUESTIONS:

[1]The Pharisees heard that Jesus was gaining and baptizing more disciples than John, [2]although in fact it was not Jesus who baptized, but his disciples. [3]When the Lord learned of this, he left Judea and went back once more to Galilee.

[4]Now he had to go through Samaria. [5]So he came to a town in Samaria called Sychar, near the plot of ground Jacob had given to his son Joseph. [6]Jacob's well was there, and Jesus, tired as he was from the journey, sat down by the well. It was about the sixth hour.

[7]When a Samaritan woman came to draw water, Jesus said to her, "Will you give me a drink?" [8](His disciples had gone into the town to buy food.)

⁹The Samaritan woman said to him, "You are a Jew and I am a Samaritan woman. How can you ask me for a drink?" (For Jews do not associate with Samaritans.)

¹⁰Jesus answered her, "If you knew the gift of God and who it is that asks you for a drink, you would have asked him and he would have given you living water."

¹¹"Sir," the woman said, "you have nothing to draw with and the well is deep. Where can you get this living water? ¹²Are you greater than our father Jacob, who gave us the well and drank from it himself, as did also his sons and his flocks and herds?"

¹³Jesus answered, "Everyone who drinks this water will be thirsty again, ¹⁴but whoever drinks the water I give him will never thirst. Indeed, the water I give him will become in him a spring of water welling up to eternal life."

¹⁵The woman said to him, "Sir, give me this water so that I won't get thirsty and have to keep coming here to draw water."

1. Why did Jews and Samaritans not get along?

2. Why do you think the Samaritan woman is alone at the well?

3. What did the woman understand by "living water"? What did Jesus mean by it?

DAY THREE READING AND QUESTIONS:

¹⁶He told her, "Go, call your husband and come back."
¹⁷"I have no husband," she replied.

Jesus said to her, "You are right when you say you have no husband. ¹⁸The fact is, you have had five husbands, and the man you now have is not your husband. What you have just said is quite true."

¹⁹"Sir," the woman said, "I can see that you are a prophet. ²⁰Our fathers worshiped on this mountain, but you Jews claim that the place where we must worship is in Jerusalem."

²¹Jesus declared, "Believe me, woman, a time is coming when you will worship the Father neither on this mountain nor in Jerusalem. ²²You Samaritans worship what you do not know; we worship what we do know, for salvation is from the Jews. ²³Yet a time is coming and has now come when the true worshipers will worship the Father in spirit and truth, for they are the kind of worshipers the Father seeks. ²⁴God is spirit, and his worshipers must worship in spirit and in truth."

²⁵The woman said, "I know that Messiah" (called Christ) "is coming. When he comes, he will explain everything to us."

²⁶Then Jesus declared, "I who speak to you am he."

1. *Why did Jesus mention the woman's husband? Was he trying to make her feel guilty?*

2. *What does it mean to worship in spirit (or Spirit) and truth? How do you think the woman reacted to this message on worship?*

3. *This is the first time Jesus clearly says he is the Messiah. Why do you think he revealed himself to this woman?*

DAY FOUR READING AND QUESTIONS:

²⁷Just then his disciples returned and were surprised to find him talking with a woman. But no one asked, "What do you want?" or "Why are you talking with her?"

²⁸Then, leaving her water jar, the woman went back to the town and said to the people, ²⁹"Come, see a man who told me everything I

ever did. Could this be the Christ?" [30]They came out of the town and made their way toward him.

[31]Meanwhile his disciples urged him, "Rabbi, eat something."

[32]But he said to them, "I have food to eat that you know nothing about."

[33]Then his disciples said to each other, "Could someone have brought him food?"

[34]"My food," said Jesus, "is to do the will of him who sent me and to finish his work. [35]Do you not say, 'Four months more and then the harvest'? I tell you, open your eyes and look at the fields! They are ripe for harvest. [36]Even now the reaper draws his wages, even now he harvests the crop for eternal life, so that the sower and the reaper may be glad together. [37]Thus the saying 'One sows and another reaps' is true. [38]I sent you to reap what you have not worked for. Others have done the hard work, and you have reaped the benefits of their labor."

[39]Many of the Samaritans from that town believed in him because of the woman's testimony, "He told me everything I ever did." [40]So when the Samaritans came to him, they urged him to stay with them, and he stayed two days. [41]And because of his words many more became believers.

[42]They said to the woman, "We no longer believe just because of what you said; now we have heard for ourselves, and we know that this man really is the Savior of the world."

1. Why did the disciples not ask Jesus why he was talking to the woman?

2. What was food for Jesus? What does this mean?

3. It seems that few in Jerusalem believed in Jesus but many in Samaria did. Why?

DAY FIVE READING AND QUESTIONS:

Go back and read the entire passage.

1. What are the ways water is used in this passage?

2. Who gives testimony to Jesus in this passage? Is their testimony believed?

3. What do the different descriptions of Jesus in this passage (bridegroom, the one from above, Son, Messiah, and Savior of the world) tell us about him?

MEDITATION ON JOHN 3:22-4:42

All they wanted was water. They wanted the baptism of John. They couldn't understand how John could let this Jesus outdo him in popularity.

John understands. He is at most the best man. Jesus is the groom. "He must become greater; I must become less."

All she wanted was water.

She found much more. A man, a Jew who spoke freely to her, a Samaritan.

A man who somehow knew her and knew about her husband (or lack of one).

"We hear Messiah's coming," she said, trying to keep the conversation away from her marital status.

"He's here. He speaks to you."

And with those words, Jesus changes this woman's life forever.

A chance meeting. An ordinary conversation. A safe topic. Water. The kind of thing that happens every day.

Jesus came to seek and save the lost. He begins the conversation. He asks for her help. For water. Somewhere along the line the conversation reverses. He doesn't ask, he gives. Earlier he had turned water to wine. Now he turns water into something even greater. Living water. Not the kind that gives life but has to be replenished, but the Holy Spirit who gives life once for all.

All they wanted was food, so the disciples go to town to buy some. Returning, they offer some to Jesus.

"No thanks," Jesus says, "I've already eaten. I have food you don't know about."

"How can that be?" the disciples say to each other. "Did someone bring him food while we were gone? Is that why he was talking with the woman?"

"My food," Jesus said, "is to do the will of the one who sent me and to finish his work. If you want food, then look. The fields are ready to be reaped. Others planted, but you will eat the crop."

Jesus isn't talking about harvesting wheat, but harvesting people. And that harvest comes. The Samaritans in town listen to the woman's testimony. They go out to the well, bring him back to the village, and he stays with them two days, telling them more about living water. Many become believers. They tell the woman, "It's not just your testimony that convinces us. Now we have heard him with our own ears and know he is the Savior of the world."

We are the disciples. We are this woman at the well. We come to Jesus asking little: drink, food, health, prosperity. We don't know whom we're asking. We can't hide the facts of our lives from him. He offers more than we ask. We want water, he gives the Spirit. We want food, he gives his Body. We want our immediate needs met, he gives a lifelong relationship.

We need to want more.

"Loving Jesus, give us living water. Feed us with the desire to do God's will. May you become greater while we become less."

HEALING AND PERSECUTION

(John 4:43-5:47)

Day One Reading and Questions:

⁴³After the two days he left for Galilee. ⁴⁴(Now Jesus himself had pointed out that a prophet has no honor in his own country.) ⁴⁵When he arrived in Galilee, the Galileans welcomed him. They had seen all that he had done in Jerusalem at the Passover Feast, for they also had been there.

⁴⁶Once more he visited Cana in Galilee, where he had turned the water into wine. And there was a certain royal official whose son lay sick at Capernaum. ⁴⁷When this man heard that Jesus had arrived in Galilee from Judea, he went to him and begged him to come and heal his son, who was close to death.

⁴⁸"Unless you people see miraculous signs and wonders," Jesus told him, "you will never believe."

⁴⁹The royal official said, "Sir, come down before my child dies."

⁵⁰Jesus replied, "You may go. Your son will live."

The man took Jesus at his word and departed. ⁵¹While he was still on the way, his servants met him with the news that his boy was living. ⁵²When he inquired as to the time when his son got better, they said to him, "The fever left him yesterday at the seventh hour."

[53]Then the father realized that this was the exact time at which Jesus had said to him, "Your son will live." So he and all his household believed. [54]This was the second miraculous sign that Jesus performed, having come from Judea to Galilee.

1. *If a prophet has no honor in his own country, why did the Galileans welcome him?*

2. *Jesus told the royal official, "Unless you people see miraculous signs and wonders you will never believe." Was Jesus condemning the man for wanting his child healed? Why did Jesus say this?*

3. *How did this official show faith in Jesus?*

DAY TWO READING AND QUESTIONS:

[1]Some time later, Jesus went up to Jerusalem for a feast of the Jews. [2]Now there is in Jerusalem near the Sheep Gate a pool, which in Aramaic is called Bethesda and which is surrounded by five covered colonnades. [3]Here a great number of disabled people used to lie—the blind, the lame, the paralyzed. [5]One who was there had been an invalid for thirty-eight years. [6]When Jesus saw him lying there and learned that he had been in this condition for a long time, he asked him, "Do you want to get well?"

[7]"Sir," the invalid replied, "I have no one to help me into the pool when the water is stirred. While I am trying to get in, someone else goes down ahead of me."

[8]Then Jesus said to him, "Get up! Pick up your mat and walk." [9]At once the man was cured; he picked up his mat and walked.

The day on which this took place was a Sabbath, [10]and so the

Jews said to the man who had been healed, "It is the Sabbath; the law forbids you to carry your mat."

[11]But he replied, "The man who made me well said to me, 'Pick up your mat and walk.'"

[12]So they asked him, "Who is this fellow who told you to pick it up and walk?"

[13]The man who was healed had no idea who it was, for Jesus had slipped away into the crowd that was there.

[14]Later Jesus found him at the temple and said to him, "See, you are well again. Stop sinning or something worse may happen to you." [15]The man went away and told the Jews that it was Jesus who had made him well.

1. *Jesus asks the man, "Do you want to get well?" Is that a strange question? Is it possible the man did not want to be well?*

2. *The man didn't even know who had healed him. What does that tell you about the man?*

3. *After Jesus finds the man again, the man tells the Jews who healed him. Why did he do this?*

Day Three Reading and Questions:

[16]So, because Jesus was doing these things on the Sabbath, the Jews persecuted him. [17]Jesus said to them, "My Father is always at his work to this very day, and I, too, am working." [18]For this reason the Jews tried all the harder to kill him; not only was he breaking the Sabbath, but he was even calling God his own Father, making himself equal with God.

[19]Jesus gave them this answer: "I tell you the truth, the Son can do nothing by himself; he can do only what he sees his Father doing, because whatever the Father does the Son also does. [20]For the Father loves the Son and shows him all he does. Yes, to your amazement he will show him even greater things than these. [21]For just as the Father raises the dead and gives them life, even so the Son gives life to whom he is pleased to give it. [22]Moreover, the Father judges no one, but has entrusted all judgment to the Son, [23]that all may honor the Son just as they honor the Father. He who does not honor the Son does not honor the Father, who sent him.

[24]"I tell you the truth, whoever hears my word and believes him who sent me has eternal life and will not be condemned; he has crossed over from death to life. [25]I tell you the truth, a time is coming and has now come when the dead will hear the voice of the Son of God and those who hear will live. [26]For as the Father has life in himself, so he has granted the Son to have life in himself. [27]And he has given him authority to judge because he is the Son of Man.

[28]"Do not be amazed at this, for a time is coming when all who are in their graves will hear his voice [29]and come out—those who have done good will rise to live, and those who have done evil will rise to be condemned. [30]By myself I can do nothing; I judge only as I hear, and my judgment is just, for I seek not to please myself but him who sent me.

1. *What was the result of the man pointing out Jesus to the Jewish leaders?*

2. *By calling God "Father" was Jesus making himself equal to God? Don't we call God "Father"? Are we equal to God?*

3. *Jesus here says he will raise the dead. By what power will he do this? When will he do this?*

Day Four Reading and Questions:

[31]"If I testify about myself, my testimony is not valid. [32]There is another who testifies in my favor, and I know that his testimony about me is valid.

[33]"You have sent to John and he has testified to the truth. [34]Not that I accept human testimony; but I mention it that you may be saved. [35]John was a lamp that burned and gave light, and you chose for a time to enjoy his light.

[36]"I have testimony weightier than that of John. For the very work that the Father has given me to finish, and which I am doing, testifies that the Father has sent me. [37]And the Father who sent me has himself testified concerning me. You have never heard his voice nor seen his form, [38]nor does his word dwell in you, for you do not believe the one he sent. [39]You diligently study the Scriptures because you think that by them you possess eternal life. These are the Scriptures that testify about me, [40]yet you refuse to come to me to have life.

[41]"I do not accept praise from men, [42]but I know you. I know that you do not have the love of God in your hearts. [43]I have come in my Father's name, and you do not accept me; but if someone else comes in his own name, you will accept him. [44]How can you believe if you accept praise from one another, yet make no effort to obtain the praise that comes from the only God?

[45]"But do not think I will accuse you before the Father. Your accuser is Moses, on whom your hopes are set. [46]If you believed Moses, you would believe me, for he wrote about me. [47]But since you do not believe what he wrote, how are you going to believe what I say?"

1. List the five persons and things that testify to Jesus in this section. Why does Jesus multiply such testimony?

2. *Is it possible today to know the Scriptures but miss Jesus? How do some (perhaps including us) do this?*

3. *What is the relationship between knowing the Scripture, coming to Jesus, and having the love of God in our hearts?*

DAY FIVE READING AND QUESTIONS:

Go back and read the entire passage.

1. *What similarities do you see between the man at the Bethesda pool and the Jewish leaders as far as their relationship with Jesus?*

2. *What is the relationship between Jesus and the Father? How is our relationship with God similar to that of Jesus? How is it different?*

3. *Why does Jesus heal the man on the Sabbath? Did he know he would get in trouble? Why are the Jewish leaders so angry at Jesus? What is at stake for them?*

MEDITATION ON JOHN 4:43-5:47

He looks like a man of faith.

He only wants his son healed. Even when Jesus warns against seeking signs, he persists in his request. When Jesus says, "Your son will live," he takes him at his word.

He seems like the biggest jerk in the Bible.

Perhaps that's a harsh assessment, but it's the way he looks to me. He first appears as an object of pity. For thirty-eight years he had been paralyzed. Imagine. Unable to move. Dependent on others for help. Not able to do anything for yourself.

Until the day a stranger came by.

"Get up and walk," the stranger said.

So he did.

For the first time in thirty-eight years, he stood up. He grabbed his mat and headed for home, not taking the time to thank the stranger or even find out his name.

Then he got in trouble.

"You, there," a man said, "what do you think you're doing?"

"Huh?" said the former paralytic.

"Don't you know it's against the law to carry your mat like that on the Sabbath?"

"But the man told me to."

"What man?"

"I don't know."

And so he didn't. Until Jesus found him again in the temple and warned him that there was something worse than paralysis. "Don't sin anymore or something worse may happen to you," Jesus said. So the man learned the name of his healer.

Did he stop and thank Jesus? Did he confess himself a sinner and ask Jesus to forgive? Did he proclaim to others what Christ had done for him? Did he invite him home with him?

No.

What did he do? He told on him! Going back to the Jews who had accused him of breaking the law, the healed man said, "I've got the name of the culprit now, the one who doesn't respect the Sabbath. His name is Jesus."

They act like crazy men. They began to persecute Jesus and even tried to kill him. How could they know their Bibles and not see God at work in this great miraculous sign?

How about us? Do we take Jesus at his word? Do we take Jesus for granted? Or do we oppose the work of Jesus because he does not do things in Bible ways (at least not how we understand the Bible)?

Yet in our bitterest moments, our most selfish times, our most ungrateful days, Jesus can and does heal us too. We least deserve his power and his forgiveness. Out of his compassion and grace, he still freely gives.

But the healing comes with a warning: "Sin no more." We must not remain as this jerk, repaying Jesus' kindness with indifference and persecution. We must not be like the Jewish leaders who think they know the Bible, but don't know Jesus. He has awakened us from the nightmare of our paralysis of sin, and we must learn his name, fall down at his feet in gratitude, and serve him evermore. We must take him at his word.

"Compassionate Lord, may we always know the one who has healed us. May we see you in the Scriptures. May we take you at your word."

HUNGER AND BREAD

(John 6:1-40)

DAY ONE READING AND QUESTIONS:

[1]Some time after this, Jesus crossed to the far shore of the Sea of Galilee (that is, the Sea of Tiberias), [2]and a great crowd of people followed him because they saw the miraculous signs he had performed on the sick. [3]Then Jesus went up on a mountainside and sat down with his disciples. [4]The Jewish Passover Feast was near.

[5]When Jesus looked up and saw a great crowd coming toward him, he said to Philip, "Where shall we buy bread for these people to eat?" [6]He asked this only to test him, for he already had in mind what he was going to do.

[7]Philip answered him, "Eight months' wages would not buy enough bread for each one to have a bite!"

[8]Another of his disciples, Andrew, Simon Peter's brother, spoke up, [9]"Here is a boy with five small barley loaves and two small fish, but how far will they go among so many?"

[10]Jesus said, "Have the people sit down." There was plenty of grass in that place, and the men sat down, about five thousand of them. [11]Jesus then took the loaves, gave thanks, and distributed to those who were seated as much as they wanted. He did the same with the fish.

[12]When they had all had enough to eat, he said to his disciples, "Gather the pieces that are left over. Let nothing be wasted." [13]So they

gathered them and filled twelve baskets with the pieces of the five barley loaves left over by those who had eaten.

> 1. Why did the crowd follow Jesus? What did they expect from him? Why do people follow Jesus today? What do we expect from him?

> 2. Contrast the reaction of Philip and of Andrew to the problem of feeding the crowd. Why did each react that way?

> 3. Is it significant that all this took place around the time of Passover? What happened at Passover?

Day Two Reading and Questions:

[14]After the people saw the miraculous sign that Jesus did, they began to say, "Surely this is the Prophet who is to come into the world." [15]Jesus, knowing that they intended to come and make him king by force, withdrew again to a mountain by himself.

[16]When evening came, his disciples went down to the lake, [17]where they got into a boat and set off across the lake for Capernaum. By now it was dark, and Jesus had not yet joined them. [18]A strong wind was blowing and the waters grew rough. [19]When they had rowed three or three and a half miles, they saw Jesus approaching the boat, walking on the water; and they were terrified. [20]But he said to them, "It is I; don't be afraid." [21]Then they were willing to take him into the boat, and immediately the boat reached the shore where they were heading.

> 1. Why would the people want to make Jesus king? What kind of king did they want? Why did they try to do this immediately after the feeding of the 5000?

2. Why did Jesus withdraw to the mountain by himself? What did Jesus usually do on mountains? Why did he especially need to be alone now?

3. Why were the disciples terrified when they saw Jesus walking on the water? Had they not just witnessed him miraculously feeding the 5000?

Day Three Reading and Questions:

[22]The next day the crowd that had stayed on the opposite shore of the lake realized that only one boat had been there, and that Jesus had not entered it with his disciples, but that they had gone away alone. [23]Then some boats from Tiberias landed near the place where the people had eaten the bread after the Lord had given thanks. [24]Once the crowd realized that neither Jesus nor his disciples were there, they got into the boats and went to Capernaum in search of Jesus.

[25]When they found him on the other side of the lake, they asked him, "Rabbi, when did you get here?"

[26]Jesus answered, "I tell you the truth, you are looking for me, not because you saw miraculous signs but because you ate the loaves and had your fill. [27]Do not work for food that spoils, but for food that endures to eternal life, which the Son of Man will give you. On him God the Father has placed his seal of approval."

1. Why did the crowd go to such lengths to find Jesus?

2. Should we look for Jesus because we want miracles? Because we want food? Why should we look for him?

3. What is the food that endures?

Day Four Reading and Questions:

28Then they asked him, "What must we do to do the works God requires?"

29Jesus answered, "The work of God is this: to believe in the one he has sent."

30So they asked him, "What miraculous sign then will you give that we may see it and believe you? What will you do? 31Our forefathers ate the manna in the desert; as it is written: 'He gave them bread from heaven to eat.'"

32Jesus said to them, "I tell you the truth, it is not Moses who has given you the bread from heaven, but it is my Father who gives you the true bread from heaven. 33For the bread of God is he who comes down from heaven and gives life to the world."

34"Sir," they said, "from now on give us this bread."

35Then Jesus declared, "I am the bread of life. He who comes to me will never go hungry, and he who believes in me will never be thirsty. 36But as I told you, you have seen me and still you do not believe. 37All that the Father gives me will come to me, and whoever comes to me I will never drive away. 38For I have come down from heaven not to do my will but to do the will of him who sent me. 39And this is the will of him who sent me, that I shall lose none of all that he has given me, but raise them up at the last day. 40For my Father's will is that everyone who looks to the Son and believes in him shall have eternal life, and I will raise him up at the last day."

1. Why do they ask what work they must do? How did Jesus respond to their question about work? Is believing work?

2. How ridiculous is it that this group demanded a sign from Jesus? What sign had they just experienced? Why did they ask for another?

3. How is Jesus the bread from heaven? How do we eat that bread?

DAY FIVE READING AND QUESTIONS:

Go back and read the entire passage.

1. What comes to mind when you think of bread? How important is bread to most people in the world?

2. How could these people see all the miracles Jesus performed and still not believe in him? Do miracles automatically create faith? What does create faith?

3. Some believe in Jesus as prophet and king, but still do not understand why he came into the world. Is it possible today to believe in Jesus and still not understand who he is? How can this be done?

MEDITATION ON JOHN 6:1-40

We all have hungers. Deep, true hungers. We hunger for food, for friendship, for understanding, for meaning, for belonging. To be human is to hunger. Jesus knows what it's like to be hungry, so he feeds the hungry. He fills all hungers.

Are we satisfied with Jesus? Or do we hunger for all the other things that promise to satisfy? They promise, but can't deliver. Jesus feeds and we never go hungry.

We are disciples. We follow Jesus. Of course we are satisfied with him. How do we express that satisfaction? We begin by talking back to our televisions. When we see those ads for products that claim to satisfy, we laugh and say, "Who do you think you're fooling? Buying you will make me no happier. Only One satisfies."

What else do we do? We intentionally refuse to buy. Why? Because those things are bad? No, because we need to learn the lesson Jesus learned in the wilderness. There was nothing evil about the bread Jesus wanted. He still didn't change the stones. Why? Because he remembered what really satisfies. If we chose to deprive ourselves of certain things we too will be reminded of what satisfies. We will discover our true hunger. We want Jesus, not some new thing.

We talk back to TV. We say no to certain purchases. We must do more. We must pass true values on to our children. We must learn and then teach by our lives what is of true value. We are hungry. Nothing on earth satisfies. Only the Word of God made flesh. The crowd is in a deserted place. There's nowhere they can go to get bread. One alone can feed them. He does. He gives them more than they can eat.

Jesus knows what it is like to be hungry. He teaches us how to be hungry.

Jesus really satisfies.

"Lord Jesus, we are racked with hungers. Make us hungry for God alone."

FLESH AND BLOOD

(John 6:41-71)

Day One Reading and Questions:

⁴¹At this the Jews began to grumble about him because he said, "I am the bread that came down from heaven." ⁴²They said, "Is this not Jesus, the son of Joseph, whose father and mother we know? How can he now say, 'I came down from heaven'?"

⁴³"Stop grumbling among yourselves," Jesus answered. ⁴⁴"No one can come to me unless the Father who sent me draws him, and I will raise him up at the last day. ⁴⁵It is written in the Prophets: 'They will all be taught by God.' Everyone who listens to the Father and learns from him comes to me. ⁴⁶No one has seen the Father except the one who is from God; only he has seen the Father. ⁴⁷I tell you the truth, he who believes has everlasting life. ⁴⁸I am the bread of life. ⁴⁹Your forefathers ate the manna in the desert, yet they died. ⁵⁰But here is the bread that comes down from heaven, which a man may eat and not die. ⁵¹I am the living bread that came down from heaven. If anyone eats of this bread, he will live forever. This bread is my flesh, which I will give for the life of the world."

1. *What does it mean when Jesus says he came down from heaven? Why did some grumble at this?*

2. *What is the relationship between Jesus as the bread from heaven and everyone being taught by God? How is teaching like bread?*

3. *Why is it significant that Jesus is living bread?*

Day Two Reading and Questions:

[52]Then the Jews began to argue sharply among themselves, "How can this man give us his flesh to eat?"

[53]Jesus said to them, "I tell you the truth, unless you eat the flesh of the Son of Man and drink his blood, you have no life in you. [54]Whoever eats my flesh and drinks my blood has eternal life, and I will raise him up at the last day. [55]For my flesh is real food and my blood is real drink. [56]Whoever eats my flesh and drinks my blood remains in me, and I in him. [57]Just as the living Father sent me and I live because of the Father, so the one who feeds on me will live because of me. [58]This is the bread that came down from heaven. Your forefathers ate manna and died, but he who feeds on this bread will live forever." [59]He said this while teaching in the synagogue in Capernaum.

1. *What did Jesus mean by eating his flesh and drinking his blood? What did his listeners think he meant?*

2. *What does it mean to feed on Jesus? How do we feed on him?*

3. *What else had Jesus done in Capernaum? Is it significant that those who misunderstood him were from Capernaum?*

Day Three Reading and Questions:

[60]On hearing it, many of his disciples said, "This is a hard teaching. Who can accept it?"

[61]Aware that his disciples were grumbling about this, Jesus said to them, "Does this offend you? [62]What if you see the Son of Man ascend to where he was before! [63]The Spirit gives life; the flesh counts for nothing. The words I have spoken to you are spirit and they are life. [64]Yet there are some of you who do not believe." For Jesus had known from the beginning which of them did not believe and who would betray him. [65]He went on to say, "This is why I told you that no one can come to me unless the Father has enabled him."

1. *Why did some disciples think this teaching on eating flesh and drinking blood was a hard teaching? What do you think is the hardest teaching of Jesus?*

2. *How are the words of Jesus Spirit and life? How are the words of Jesus related to the Holy Spirit?*

3. *What does it mean that no one can come to Jesus unless the Father enables him? Are we predestined to believe or not believe? What part does God play in creating faith?*

Day Four Reading and Questions:

[66]From this time many of his disciples turned back and no longer followed him.

[67]"You do not want to leave too, do you?" Jesus asked the Twelve.

[68]Simon Peter answered him, "Lord, to whom shall we go? You have the words of eternal life. [69]We believe and know that you are the Holy One of God."

[70]Then Jesus replied, "Have I not chosen you, the Twelve? Yet one of you is a devil!" [71](He meant Judas, the son of Simon Iscariot, who, though one of the Twelve, was later to betray him.)

1. *Are the teachings of Jesus too hard? Do we sometimes try to make the teachings of Jesus too easy?*

2. *Why does Peter stay with Jesus? Why do we?*

3. *Why did Jesus choose Judas if he was a devil?*

Day Five Reading and Questions:

Go back and read the entire passage.

1. *How does eating the flesh and drinking the blood of Jesus relate to the Lord's Supper? Is the flesh and blood of Jesus really present in the Supper? How?*

2. *Do we ever stop following Jesus because we think his teachings are too hard? What do you think is the hardest teaching of Jesus?*

3. *Do we ever have trouble believing that Jesus was flesh and blood just as we are?*

MEDITATION ON 6:41-71

We eat the flesh and drink the blood of Jesus. Such language is familiar to us. But to those first hearers it must have been shocking and disgusting. With language like this, no wonder some later would accuse Christians of being cannibals!

So what does it mean to eat the flesh of Jesus and drink his blood? Surely we cannot hear these words without thinking of the Lord's Supper. There we participate (or commune, as in communion) in the flesh and blood of Jesus (see I Corinthians 10:16). We become one with Jesus. We experience his body and blood given for us. We have unity with others in the one body of Jesus, his spiritual body of believers.

Eating flesh and drinking blood means even more. It means God teaches us and we listen to him. It means trusting in Jesus—his words, his life, his body given for us. It means we receive life not from physical bread alone, not from anything or anyone this world can offer. We find our food, our drink, our life in Jesus alone.

Some are offended by Jesus' words, perhaps because they took him literally. They find them so hard they no longer follow him. But these are hard words. Not just hard to understand but hard to do. We are willing to eat the flesh of Jesus and drink his blood. But at the same time we try countless other ways to find nourishment and life—food, family, pleasure, success—the list goes on and on.

Do we trust Jesus enough to feed only on him? To believe that he alone is the source of life?

"Lord Jesus, increase our faith. May we feed on you alone so you may be in us and we in you.

TEACHING AND DIVISION
(John 7:1-53)

DAY ONE READING AND QUESTIONS:

¹After this, Jesus went around in Galilee, purposely staying away from Judea because the Jews there were waiting to take his life. ²But when the Jewish Feast of Tabernacles was near, ³Jesus' brothers said to him, "You ought to leave here and go to Judea, so that your disciples may see the miracles you do. ⁴No one who wants to become a public figure acts in secret. Since you are doing these things, show yourself to the world." ⁵For even his own brothers did not believe in him.

⁶Therefore Jesus told them, "The right time for me has not yet come; for you any time is right. ⁷The world cannot hate you, but it hates me because I testify that what it does is evil. ⁸You go to the Feast. I am not yet going up to this Feast, because for me the right time has not yet come." ⁹Having said this, he stayed in Galilee.

¹⁰However, after his brothers had left for the Feast, he went also, not publicly, but in secret. ¹¹Now at the Feast the Jews were watching for him and asking, "Where is that man?"

¹²Among the crowds there was widespread whispering about him. Some said, "He is a good man."

Others replied, "No, he deceives the people." ¹³But no one would say anything publicly about him for fear of the Jews.

1. Why did the brothers of Jesus want him to go to Jerusalem? Why didn't Jesus want to go? Why do you think the brothers of Jesus did not believe in him?

2. What does Jesus mean by "the time is not right"? Why does he say he is not going to Jerusalem and then change his mind and go? Was the time suddenly right?

3. Why did Jesus go to Jerusalem in secret? Does this have something to do with the different opinions about him among the crowds?

Day Two Reading and Questions:

[14]Not until halfway through the Feast did Jesus go up to the temple courts and begin to teach. [15]The Jews were amazed and asked, "How did this man get such learning without having studied?"

[16]Jesus answered, "My teaching is not my own. It comes from him who sent me. [17]If anyone chooses to do God's will, he will find out whether my teaching comes from God or whether I speak on my own. [18]He who speaks on his own does so to gain honor for himself, but he who works for the honor of the one who sent him is a man of truth; there is nothing false about him. [19]Has not Moses given you the law? Yet not one of you keeps the law. Why are you trying to kill me?"

[20]"You are demon-possessed," the crowd answered. "Who is trying to kill you?"

[21]Jesus said to them, "I did one miracle, and you are all astonished. [22]Yet, because Moses gave you circumcision (though actually it did not come from Moses, but from the patriarchs), you circumcise a child on the Sabbath. [23]Now if a child can be circumcised on the Sabbath so that the law of Moses may not be broken, why are you

angry with me for healing the whole man on the Sabbath? ²⁴Stop judging by mere appearances, and make a right judgment."

> 1. *Did Jesus have to study to understand the Scriptures? If not, how is he human like we are? If so, what does the crowd mean when it says he did not study?*
>
> 2. *How can one test whether or not Jesus speaks from God?*
>
> 3. *The crowd marvels at the teaching of Jesus, then later says he has a demon. What does this tell you about the crowd?*

Day Three Reading and Questions:

²⁵At that point some of the people of Jerusalem began to ask, "Isn't this the man they are trying to kill? ²⁶Here he is, speaking publicly, and they are not saying a word to him. Have the authorities really concluded that he is the Christ? ²⁷But we know where this man is from; when the Christ comes, no one will know where he is from."

²⁸Then Jesus, still teaching in the temple courts, cried out, "Yes, you know me, and you know where I am from. I am not here on my own, but he who sent me is true. You do not know him, ²⁹but I know him because I am from him and he sent me."

³⁰At this they tried to seize him, but no one laid a hand on him, because his time had not yet come. ³¹Still, many in the crowd put their faith in him. They said, "When the Christ comes, will he do more miraculous signs than this man?"

³²The Pharisees heard the crowd whispering such things about him. Then the chief priests and the Pharisees sent temple guards to arrest him.

³³Jesus said, "I am with you for only a short time, and then I go to the one who sent me. ³⁴You will look for me, but you will not find me; and where I am, you cannot come."

³⁵The Jews said to one another, "Where does this man intend to go that we cannot find him? Will he go where our people live scattered among the Greeks, and teach the Greeks? ³⁶What did he mean when he said, 'You will look for me, but you will not find me,' and 'Where I am, you cannot come'?"

³⁷On the last and greatest day of the Feast, Jesus stood and said in a loud voice, "If anyone is thirsty, let him come to me and drink. ³⁸Whoever believes in me, as the Scripture has said, streams of living water will flow from within him." ³⁹By this he meant the Spirit, whom those who believed in him were later to receive. Up to that time the Spirit had not been given, since Jesus had not yet been glorified.

1. *Why did some in the crowd find it hard to believe that Jesus was the Christ? Why did many put their faith in him?*

2. *What did Jesus mean when he spoke of going where he would not be found?*

3. *How is the Spirit like living water? Who else in John had been promised living water?*

Day Four Reading and Questions:

⁴⁰On hearing his words, some of the people said, "Surely this man is the Prophet."

⁴¹Others said, "He is the Christ."

Still others asked, "How can the Christ come from Galilee? ⁴²Does not the Scripture say that the Christ will come from David's family and from Bethlehem, the town where David lived?" [43]Thus the people were divided because of Jesus. [44]Some wanted to seize him, but no one laid a hand on him.

[45]Finally the temple guards went back to the chief priests and Pharisees, who asked them, "Why didn't you bring him in?"

[46]"No one ever spoke the way this man does," the guards declared.

[47]"You mean he has deceived you also?" the Pharisees retorted. [48]"Has any of the rulers or of the Pharisees believed in him? [49]No! But this mob that knows nothing of the law—there is a curse on them."

[50]Nicodemus, who had gone to Jesus earlier and who was one of their own number, asked, [51]"Does our law condemn anyone without first hearing him to find out what he is doing?"

[52]They replied, "Are you from Galilee, too? Look into it, and you will find that a prophet does not come out of Galilee."

[53]Then each went to his own home.

1. Why are the people divided over Jesus?

2. Why didn't the temple guard arrest Jesus?

3. Is Nicodemus a believer in Jesus or not?

Day Five Reading and Questions:

Go back and read the entire passage.

1. What are some ways today that the words of Jesus cause controversy?

2. Where did Jesus come from? Aren't there many correct answers to this question? Why is this an important question?

3. Why didn't the Pharisees and rulers believe in Jesus? Should they not have been the first to believe?

MEDITATION ON JOHN 7:1-53

Why do some find it so hard to believe in Jesus?

Even his brothers did not believe. Is it any wonder? Could you believe the brother you had grown up with was the Son of God?

The Pharisees who prided themselves on knowing and keeping the Law did not believe in him. How could they, when he violates the rules they had made for the Sabbath? Jesus thinks it is the Pharisees who have twisted the Law. They know better.

The chief priests and rulers do not believe in him. They even plot to kill him. Why? Because as much as they wanted a Messiah, they even more wanted a Messiah they could control.

Aren't we glad we live in a place and time when it is easy to believe in Jesus? Almost everyone respects him. Millions call themselves Christian. Many attend church each Sunday. Why is it easier now? Because we finally have a Messiah we can control—through churches, laws, morality, and niceness that preserves the status quo.

The crowd cannot make up its mind about Jesus. Prophet? Good man? Deceiver? We find it easier because we don't read the gospels. Or we explain them away. Or we feel religious about them and live our lives as we wish.

Nicodemus asks, "Does our law condemn anyone without first hearing him to find out what he is doing?" We might ask, "Do we really put our faith in Jesus without first hearing him to find out what he is doing?" Easy faith is no better than no faith at all.

"Lord Jesus, open our hearts, minds, and lives to who you really are. May we embrace the costly faith you call us to."

FATHER ABRAHAM AND FATHER GOD

(John 8:1-59)

DAY ONE READING AND QUESTIONS:

¹But Jesus went to the Mount of Olives. ²At dawn he appeared again in the temple courts, where all the people gathered around him, and he sat down to teach them. ³The teachers of the law and the Pharisees brought in a woman caught in adultery. They made her stand before the group ⁴and said to Jesus, "Teacher, this woman was caught in the act of adultery. ⁵In the Law Moses commanded us to stone such women. Now what do you say?" ⁶They were using this question as a trap, in order to have a basis for accusing him.

But Jesus bent down and started to write on the ground with his finger. ⁷When they kept on questioning him, he straightened up and said to them, "If any one of you is without sin, let him be the first to throw a stone at her." ⁸Again he stooped down and wrote on the ground.

⁹At this, those who heard began to go away one at a time, the older ones first, until only Jesus was left, with the woman still standing there. ¹⁰Jesus straightened up and asked her, "Woman, where are they? Has no one condemned you?"

¹¹"No one, sir," she said.

"Then neither do I condemn you," Jesus declared. "Go now and leave your life of sin."

1. Were the teachers of the law and the Pharisees concerned for the woman? Were they concerned about the Law? What was there true concern?

2. Why do you think the older ones left first after Jesus spoke of being without sin? Are those older more likely to realize they are sinners?

3. Did Jesus excuse this woman's sin? What makes you think so?

DAY TWO READING AND QUESTIONS:

[12]When Jesus spoke again to the people, he said, "I am the light of the world. Whoever follows me will never walk in darkness, but will have the light of life."

[13]The Pharisees challenged him, "Here you are, appearing as your own witness; your testimony is not valid."

[14]Jesus answered, "Even if I testify on my own behalf, my testimony is valid, for I know where I came from and where I am going. But you have no idea where I come from or where I am going. [15]You judge by human standards; I pass judgment on no one. [16]But if I do judge, my decisions are right, because I am not alone. I stand with the Father, who sent me. [17]In your own Law it is written that the testimony of two men is valid. [18]I am one who testifies for myself; my other witness is the Father, who sent me."

[19]Then they asked him, "Where is your father?"

"You do not know me or my Father," Jesus replied. "If you knew me, you would know my Father also." [20]He spoke these words while teaching in the temple area near the place where the offerings were put. Yet no one seized him, because his time had not yet come.

[21]Once more Jesus said to them, "I am going away, and you will look for me, and you will die in your sin. Where I go, you cannot come."

²²This made the Jews ask, "Will he kill himself? Is that why he says, 'Where I go, you cannot come'?"

²³But he continued, "You are from below; I am from above. You are of this world; I am not of this world. ²⁴I told you that you would die in your sins; if you do not believe that I am the one I claim to be, you will indeed die in your sins."

²⁵"Who are you?" they asked.

"Just what I have been claiming all along," Jesus replied. ²⁶"I have much to say in judgment of you. But he who sent me is reliable, and what I have heard from him I tell the world."

²⁷They did not understand that he was telling them about his Father. ²⁸So Jesus said, "When you have lifted up the Son of Man, then you will know that I am the one I claim to be and that I do nothing on my own but speak just what the Father has taught me. ²⁹The one who sent me is with me; he has not left me alone, for I always do what pleases him." ³⁰Even as he spoke, many put their faith in him.

1. How does Jesus distinguish himself from his listeners?

2. How is the Father a witness to Jesus? How do different ones of his listeners react to that witness?

3. What does it mean to lift up the Son of Man?

Day Three Reading and Questions:

³¹To the Jews who had believed him, Jesus said, "If you hold to my teaching, you are really my disciples. ³²Then you will know the truth, and the truth will set you free."

³³They answered him, "We are Abraham's descendants and have never been slaves of anyone. How can you say that we shall be set free?"

³⁴Jesus replied, "I tell you the truth, everyone who sins is a slave to sin. ³⁵Now a slave has no permanent place in the family, but a son belongs to it forever. ³⁶So if the Son sets you free, you will be free indeed. ³⁷I know you are Abraham's descendants. Yet you are ready to kill me, because you have no room for my word. ³⁸I am telling you what I have seen in the Father's presence, and you do what you have heard from your father."

³⁹"Abraham is our father," they answered.

"If you were Abraham's children," said Jesus, "then you would do the things Abraham did. ⁴⁰As it is, you are determined to kill me, a man who has told you the truth that I heard from God. Abraham did not do such things. ⁴¹You are doing the things your own father does."

"We are not illegitimate children," they protested. "The only Father we have is God himself."

⁴²Jesus said to them, "If God were your Father, you would love me, for I came from God and now am here. I have not come on my own; but he sent me. ⁴³Why is my language not clear to you? Because you are unable to hear what I say. ⁴⁴You belong to your father, the devil, and you want to carry out your father's desire. He was a murderer from the beginning, not holding to the truth, for there is no truth in him. When he lies, he speaks his native language, for he is a liar and the father of lies. ⁴⁵Yet because I tell the truth, you do not believe me! ⁴⁶Can any of you prove me guilty of sin? If I am telling the truth, why don't you believe me? ⁴⁷He who belongs to God hears what God says. The reason you do not hear is that you do not belong to God."

1. *What were the Jews told to do in order to know the truth? Is knowing the truth a matter of having correct answers or a matter of living?*

2. *Why were these hearers offended when Jesus calls them slaves? Would we be offended if someone called us a slave? Are we slaves? Who sets us free?*

3. Why does Jesus call them children of the devil? Isn't this harsh? What had they done to deserve this?

DAY FOUR READING AND QUESTIONS:

[48]The Jews answered him, "Aren't we right in saying that you are a Samaritan and demon-possessed?"

[49]"I am not possessed by a demon," said Jesus, "but I honor my Father and you dishonor me. [50]I am not seeking glory for myself; but there is one who seeks it, and he is the judge. [51]I tell you the truth, if anyone keeps my word, he will never see death."

[52]At this the Jews exclaimed, "Now we know that you are demon-possessed! Abraham died and so did the prophets, yet you say that if anyone keeps your word, he will never taste death. [53]Are you greater than our father Abraham? He died, and so did the prophets. Who do you think you are?"

[54]Jesus replied, "If I glorify myself, my glory means nothing. My Father, whom you claim as your God, is the one who glorifies me. [55]Though you do not know him, I know him. If I said I did not, I would be a liar like you, but I do know him and keep his word. [56]Your father Abraham rejoiced at the thought of seeing my day; he saw it and was glad."

[57]"You are not yet fifty years old," the Jews said to him, "and you have seen Abraham!"

[58]"I tell you the truth," Jesus answered, "before Abraham was born, I am!" [59]At this, they picked up stones to stone him, but Jesus hid himself, slipping away from the temple grounds.

1. They call Jesus a Samaritan. Why is this an insult?

2. Earlier some in this crowd believed in Jesus. Now they say he has a demon. What changed their minds?

3. *What did Jesus say that made them want to stone him? Why did they react so violently?*

Day Five Reading and Questions:

Go back and read the entire passage.

1. *This passage refers often to "the Jews." Does this mean all the Jews? Who is this term talking about?*

2. *Does Jesus intentionally make the crowd angry by calling them slaves, children of the devil, and liars? Why would Jesus do this?*

3. *Why were these Jews so proud to have Abraham as their father (or ancestor)? Whom does Jesus point to as his Father?*

MEDITATION ON JOHN 8:1-59

"Who's your daddy?"

It's more than a taunt at a sporting event. It's a question of identity. As I get older, I increasingly see my dad in the mirror and hear his voice in words from my own mouth. Without meaning to, we resemble our fathers.

It's the same way spiritually. We have many spiritual fathers and mothers, those who passed the faith on to us, and we resemble each of them.

Abraham is our father (see Romans 4). We imitate his astounding faith. We trust God even when it makes no sense, even when he demands the impossible, just as Abraham did when he offered his son Isaac (see Genesis 22). We should be proud that Abraham is our father.

But that is not enough. Many were proud of being Abraham's children, but they would not accept Jesus. Jesus reminds them that they really have only one Father and that if they truly were God's children, they would see the family resemblance in Jesus.

We are not likely to prefer Abraham to Jesus. But it may be that other spiritual fathers and mothers—parents, churches, and traditions—can actually lead us away from Jesus. We (like some of these Jews) might prefer our comfortable religion to the difficult man from Nazareth.

The truth of Jesus is not some external objective truth available to all. Instead, only if we are his disciples and hold to his teachings will we know the truth. Only if we are willing to follow one who is lifted up on the cross will we see the light. Only if we remember that we too are sinners can we hold on the stones and not throw them.

Who's your Father? Do you resemble him?

"Father, mold us into your image, the image we see in Christ. Give us hearts of mercy, eyes that see the light, and feet that follow to the cross, so we may know and live the truth."

BLIND AND BLINDER

(John 9:1-41)

Day One Reading and Questions:

¹As he went along, he saw a man blind from birth. ²His disciples asked him, "Rabbi, who sinned, this man or his parents, that he was born blind?"

³"Neither this man nor his parents sinned," said Jesus, "but this happened so that the work of God might be displayed in his life. ⁴As long as it is day, we must do the work of him who sent me. Night is coming, when no one can work. ⁵While I am in the world, I am the light of the world."

⁶Having said this, he spit on the ground, made some mud with the saliva, and put it on the man's eyes. ⁷"Go," he told him, "wash in the Pool of Siloam" (this word means Sent). So the man went and washed, and came home seeing.

⁸His neighbors and those who had formerly seen him begging asked, "Isn't this the same man who used to sit and beg?" ⁹Some claimed that he was.

Others said, "No, he only looks like him."

But he himself insisted, "I am the man."

¹⁰"How then were your eyes opened?" they demanded.

¹¹He replied, "The man they call Jesus made some mud and put it on my eyes. He told me to go to Siloam and wash. So I went and washed, and then I could see."

¹²"Where is this man?" they asked him.

"I don't know," he said.

1. Why did the disciples think someone had sinned to make the man blind? Why does evil happen to some and not to others?

2. Jesus said this man was born blind so that the work of God might be displayed in his life. Does God make people blind? Does God send evil on us so his work might be seen?

3. How could this man lose sight of Jesus once he was healed? Does this show ingratitude on his part?

Day Two Reading and Questions:

¹³They brought to the Pharisees the man who had been blind. ¹⁴Now the day on which Jesus had made the mud and opened the man's eyes was a Sabbath. ¹⁵Therefore the Pharisees also asked him how he had received his sight. "He put mud on my eyes," the man replied, "and I washed, and now I see."

¹⁶Some of the Pharisees said, "This man is not from God, for he does not keep the Sabbath."

But others asked, "How can a sinner do such miraculous signs?" So they were divided.

¹⁷Finally they turned again to the blind man, "What have you to say about him? It was your eyes he opened."

The man replied, "He is a prophet."

¹⁸The Jews still did not believe that he had been blind and had received his sight until they sent for the man's parents. ¹⁹"Is this your son?" they asked. "Is this the one you say was born blind? How is it that now he can see?"

²⁰"We know he is our son," the parents answered, "and we know he was born blind. ²¹But how he can see now, or who opened his eyes, we don't know. Ask him. He is of age; he will speak for himself." ²²His parents said this because they were afraid of the Jews, for already the Jews had decided that anyone who acknowledged that Jesus was the Christ would be put out of the synagogue. ²³That was why his parents said, "He is of age; ask him."

1. Why weren't the Pharisees happy that the man was healed?

2. Why weren't the man's parents happier about their son's healing?

3. What does the blind man think of Jesus? Why would he think this?

Day Three Reading and Questions:

²⁴A second time they summoned the man who had been blind. "Give glory to God," they said. "We know this man is a sinner."

²⁵He replied, "Whether he is a sinner or not, I don't know. One thing I do know. I was blind but now I see!"

²⁶Then they asked him, "What did he do to you? How did he open your eyes?"

²⁷He answered, "I have told you already and you did not listen. Why do you want to hear it again? Do you want to become his disciples, too?"

²⁸Then they hurled insults at him and said, "You are this fellow's disciple! We are disciples of Moses! ²⁹We know that God spoke to Moses, but as for this fellow, we don't even know where he comes from."

³⁰The man answered, "Now that is remarkable! You don't know where he comes from, yet he opened my eyes. ³¹We know that God does not listen to sinners. He listens to the godly man who does his will. ³²Nobody has ever heard of opening the eyes of a man born blind. ³³If this man were not from God, he could do nothing."

³⁴To this they replied, "You were steeped in sin at birth; how dare you lecture us!" And they threw him out.

1. Why do the Pharisees think Jesus is a sinner?

2. Why does the man who now can see think Jesus is from God?

3. Why do the Pharisees think the former blind man is a sinner? Are the Pharisees different from the disciples of Jesus in this regard?

DAY FOUR READING AND QUESTIONS:

³⁵Jesus heard that they had thrown him out, and when he found him, he said, "Do you believe in the Son of Man?"

³⁶"Who is he, sir?" the man asked. "Tell me so that I may believe in him."

³⁷Jesus said, "You have now seen him; in fact, he is the one speaking with you."

³⁸Then the man said, "Lord, I believe," and he worshiped him.

³⁹Jesus said, "For judgment I have come into this world, so that the blind will see and those who see will become blind."

⁴⁰Some Pharisees who were with him heard him say this and asked, "What? Are we blind too?"

⁴¹Jesus said, "If you were blind, you would not be guilty of sin; but now that you claim you can see, your guilt remains."

1. Why does Jesus search for the blind man?

2. Why does the blind man worship Jesus?

3. Why do the Pharisees think Jesus is talking about them when he speaks of those who see being blind?

Day Five Reading and Questions:

Go back and read the entire passage.

1. Name all the people who are blind in this passage. Why are they blind?

2. Are we ever blind to the work of God? What makes us so?

3. How can we keep our eyes open to the work of God?

MEDITATION ON JOHN 9:1-41

It was truly a day of miracles and wonders. A wonder that a man born blind should see. A greater wonder that some could see the healing and still be blind to Jesus. But the greatest wonder is that the Son of Man came to save sinners by calling them to faith. The blind man was overjoyed to see grass and trees and flowers and his mother's face. But the greatest thing he saw that day was the face of the one who healed him, the one who came to save.

I pray we will never know what it's like to be blind. We can't really imagine what it must have been like to see for the first time. It's also hard to believe that there are still people in our world who refuse to see Jesus for who he is, who can see the powerful works of creation and redemption and fail to see the hand behind them.

Or is it hard? True, we have not been born blind. But what is worse, we have blinded ourselves to the work of Jesus. We have turned our backs on him through sin. The greatest miracle is not that Jesus healed the man born blind, but that he sought us out when we were blind to his love. He put his hands on us and healed. He told us to wash, not in the pool of Siloam, but in the waters of baptism. He heals our sins not by mud, but by his own blood. By his hand, and by that washing, and by his blood he gave us new sight, new life.

Before this miracle, Jesus tells the disciples, "I am the light of the world" (John 9:5). "Light" is one of John's favorite words for Jesus. He contrasts it with the darkness of sin. What separates Christians from the blindness of the world is not our innate niceness or our good works. We are different because we see the Light. We believe in him.

That doesn't mean we have all the answers. No one fully understands Jesus. Even we who have served him all the years of our lives must confess that we see him only dimly. But no matter how weak our faith, like the blind man we know one thing for certain.

We were blind.

Now we see.

So we worship him.

"Lord Jesus, restore our sight! May we see you, the Light of the world! We worship you as the one who heals, forgives, and enlightens."

SHEPHERD AND SHEEP

(John 10:1-42)

Day One Reading and Questions:

¹"I tell you the truth, the man who does not enter the sheep pen by the gate, but climbs in by some other way, is a thief and a robber. ²The man who enters by the gate is the shepherd of his sheep. ³The watchman opens the gate for him, and the sheep listen to his voice. He calls his own sheep by name and leads them out. ⁴When he has brought out all his own, he goes on ahead of them, and his sheep follow him because they know his voice. ⁵But they will never follow a stranger; in fact, they will run away from him because they do not recognize a stranger's voice." ⁶Jesus used this figure of speech, but they did not understand what he was telling them.

⁷Therefore Jesus said again, "I tell you the truth, I am the gate for the sheep. ⁸All who ever came before me were thieves and robbers, but the sheep did not listen to them. ⁹I am the gate; whoever enters through me will be saved. He will come in and go out, and find pasture. ¹⁰The thief comes only to steal and kill and destroy; I have come that they may have life, and have it to the full.

1. What do you know about sheep? Are they easy to care for? What challenges do they pose?

2. How is this saying like a parable?

3. Who are the thieves and robbers? Does Jesus reject all religious teachers before he came?

DAY TWO READING AND QUESTIONS:

[11]"I am the good shepherd. The good shepherd lays down his life for the sheep. [12]The hired hand is not the shepherd who owns the sheep. So when he sees the wolf coming, he abandons the sheep and runs away. Then the wolf attacks the flock and scatters it. [13]The man runs away because he is a hired hand and cares nothing for the sheep.

[14]"I am the good shepherd; I know my sheep and my sheep know me— [15]just as the Father knows me and I know the Father—and I lay down my life for the sheep. [16]I have other sheep that are not of this sheep pen. I must bring them also. They too will listen to my voice, and there shall be one flock and one shepherd. [17]The reason my Father loves me is that I lay down my life—only to take it up again. [18]No one takes it from me, but I lay it down of my own accord. I have authority to lay it down and authority to take it up again. This command I received from my Father."

[19]At these words the Jews were again divided. [20]Many of them said, "He is demon-possessed and raving mad. Why listen to him?"

[21]But others said, "These are not the sayings of a man possessed by a demon. Can a demon open the eyes of the blind?"

1. Who is the hired hand in this saying? Who might be offended by this description?

2. Who are the other sheep that are not of this sheep pen?

3. What does the good shepherd do for the sheep?

Day Three Reading and Questions:

²²Then came the Feast of Dedication at Jerusalem. It was winter, ²³and Jesus was in the temple area walking in Solomon's Colonnade. ²⁴The Jews gathered around him, saying, "How long will you keep us in suspense? If you are the Christ, tell us plainly."

²⁵Jesus answered, "I did tell you, but you do not believe. The miracles I do in my Father's name speak for me, ²⁶but you do not believe because you are not my sheep. ²⁷My sheep listen to my voice; I know them, and they follow me. ²⁸I give them eternal life, and they shall never perish; no one can snatch them out of my hand. ²⁹My Father, who has given them to me, is greater than all; no one can snatch them out of my Father's hand. ³⁰I and the Father are one."

1. Why do you think these Jews asked for a plain answer from Jesus? Had not Jesus been plain enough? Why didn't they understand his plain answer?

2. How do we show we are the sheep of Jesus?

3. What does it mean that no one can snatch the sheep from the hand of Jesus? Does this mean we can never be lost once we are sheep?

Day Four Reading and Questions:

³¹Again the Jews picked up stones to stone him, ³²but Jesus said to them, "I have shown you many great miracles from the Father. For which of these do you stone me?"

[33]"We are not stoning you for any of these," replied the Jews, "but for blasphemy, because you, a mere man, claim to be God."

[34]Jesus answered them, "Is it not written in your Law, 'I have said you are gods'? [35]If he called them 'gods,' to whom the word of God came—and the Scripture cannot be broken— [36]what about the one whom the Father set apart as his very own and sent into the world? Why then do you accuse me of blasphemy because I said, 'I am God's Son'? [37]Do not believe me unless I do what my Father does. [38]But if I do it, even though you do not believe me, believe the miracles, that you may know and understand that the Father is in me, and I in the Father." [39]Again they tried to seize him, but he escaped their grasp.

[40]Then Jesus went back across the Jordan to the place where John had been baptizing in the early days. Here he stayed [41]and many people came to him. They said, "Though John never performed a miraculous sign, all that John said about this man was true." [42]And in that place many believed in Jesus.

1. How did Jesus claim to be God?

2. Are we sons (or daughters) of God? If so, how? If so, how are we different from Jesus?

3. How can one tell that someone is God's son?

DAY FIVE READING AND QUESTIONS:

Go back and read the entire passage.

1. What comes to mind when you think of Jesus as the good shepherd? Is this a comforting picture? A challenging one?

2. Why do some accuse Jesus of having a demon and others want to stone him? Aren't these extreme reactions to the Good Shepherd?

3. Why should those who heard Jesus believe in him? Why should we?

MEDITATION ON JOHN 10:1-42

As I write this I look at a picture of Jesus as the good shepherd. He holds his staff in one hand, raises the other hand in blessing, and gazes out at me with a look of calm gentleness. Behind him the sheep peacefully sleep or graze.

It's nice as a Sunday School picture or even an icon, but far from the reality of being a shepherd.

Shepherds were the cowboys of Jesus' world (without the romance Americans associate with cowboys). Shepherds were nomads, drifters, many times thieves and outlaws. It's shocking that Jesus calls himself a shepherd.

Sheep are also different in reality than in our imagination. We think of them as clean, soft, cute puffy balls of cotton.

Sheep are prone to wander off, get lost, and hurt themselves. I think I live in a world of sheep.

Sheep don't know enough to get out of the rain. When the wolf comes, they clump together to make it easy for him to destroy them all. I think I'm part of a church of sheep.

Sheep are dumb, headstrong, and smelly. I think I am a sheep.

At one level it is no compliment for Jesus to call us sheep. We would rather think of ourselves as lions, bears, or wolves. There is no sports team named "The Sheep." Rams perhaps, but not helpless sheep.

But that is what we are. With all our pretence of having our lives together and knowing exactly where we are going, we are in reality prone to getting lost.

We need a shepherd. One who guides and protects. One who will give his life for us. We need a place of safety in a world of terror. The door to that place of safety, that fold for the sheep, is Jesus himself. He is the shepherd.

We dare not try to direct our own lives. We will get lost. We dare not try to find our own pasture and water. Only one gives daily bread. We dare not presume we can create our own security. One gave himself for us.

He knows us by name. He calls. We hear and follow.

"Good Shepherd, help us admit that we are sheep. Open our ears to hear your voice and follow. May we live today in confidence that no one can snatch us from you."

DEATH AND RESURRECTION

(John 11:1-57)

Day One Reading and Questions:

¹Now a man named Lazarus was sick. He was from Bethany, the village of Mary and her sister Martha. ²This Mary, whose brother Lazarus now lay sick, was the same one who poured perfume on the Lord and wiped his feet with her hair. ³So the sisters sent word to Jesus, "Lord, the one you love is sick."

⁴When he heard this, Jesus said, "This sickness will not end in death. No, it is for God's glory so that God's Son may be glorified through it." ⁵Jesus loved Martha and her sister and Lazarus. ⁶Yet when he heard that Lazarus was sick, he stayed where he was two more days.

⁷Then he said to his disciples, "Let us go back to Judea."

⁸"But Rabbi," they said, "a short while ago the Jews tried to stone you, and yet you are going back there?"

⁹Jesus answered, "Are there not twelve hours of daylight? A man who walks by day will not stumble, for he sees by this world's light. ¹⁰It is when he walks by night that he stumbles, for he has no light."

¹¹After he had said this, he went on to tell them, "Our friend Lazarus has fallen asleep; but I am going there to wake him up."

¹²His disciples replied, "Lord, if he sleeps, he will get better." ¹³Jesus had been speaking of his death, but his disciples thought he meant natural sleep.

[14]So then he told them plainly, "Lazarus is dead, [15]and for your sake I am glad I was not there, so that you may believe. But let us go to him."

[16]Then Thomas (called Didymus) said to the rest of the disciples, "Let us also go, that we may die with him."

1. *If Jesus truly loved Lazarus, why didn't he immediately go to heal him? Shouldn't we want those we love to be immediately healed?*

2. *Why didn't the disciples want Jesus to go back to Judea? How does Jesus answer their concern?*

3. *What does Thomas mean by his statement? Does he want to die with Lazarus? With Jesus? Why?*

Day Two Reading and Questions:

[17]On his arrival, Jesus found that Lazarus had already been in the tomb for four days. [18]Bethany was less than two miles from Jerusalem, [19]and many Jews had come to Martha and Mary to comfort them in the loss of their brother. [20]When Martha heard that Jesus was coming, she went out to meet him, but Mary stayed at home.

[21]"Lord," Martha said to Jesus, "if you had been here, my brother would not have died. [22]But I know that even now God will give you whatever you ask."

[23]Jesus said to her, "Your brother will rise again."

[24]Martha answered, "I know he will rise again in the resurrection at the last day."

[25]Jesus said to her, "I am the resurrection and the life. He who believes in me will live, even though he dies; [26]and whoever lives and believes in me will never die. Do you believe this?"

²⁷"Yes, Lord," she told him, "I believe that you are the Christ, the Son of God, who was to come into the world."

²⁸And after she had said this, she went back and called her sister Mary aside. "The Teacher is here," she said, "and is asking for you." ²⁹When Mary heard this, she got up quickly and went to him. ³⁰Now Jesus had not yet entered the village, but was still at the place where Martha had met him. ³¹When the Jews who had been with Mary in the house, comforting her, noticed how quickly she got up and went out, they followed her, supposing she was going to the tomb to mourn there.

³²When Mary reached the place where Jesus was and saw him, she fell at his feet and said, "Lord, if you had been here, my brother would not have died."

1. *Both Martha and Mary say Lazarus would not have died if Jesus had been there. Were they disappointed in Jesus? Hurt by his absence? Or were they expressing their faith in him?*

2. *Does Martha expect Jesus to raise Lazarus from the dead? Should she have expected it?*

3. *Martha confesses that Jesus is the Christ, the Son of God. Does she believe he is also the resurrection and the life?*

Day Three Reading and Questions:

³³When Jesus saw her weeping, and the Jews who had come along with her also weeping, he was deeply moved in spirit and troubled. ³⁴"Where have you laid him?" he asked.

"Come and see, Lord," they replied.

³⁵Jesus wept.

³⁶Then the Jews said, "See how he loved him!"

37But some of them said, "Could not he who opened the eyes of the blind man have kept this man from dying?"

38Jesus, once more deeply moved, came to the tomb. It was a cave with a stone laid across the entrance. 39"Take away the stone," he said. "But, Lord," said Martha, the sister of the dead man, "by this time there is a bad odor, for he has been there four days."

40Then Jesus said, "Did I not tell you that if you believed, you would see the glory of God?"

41So they took away the stone. Then Jesus looked up and said, "Father, I thank you that you have heard me. 42I knew that you always hear me, but I said this for the benefit of the people standing here, that they may believe that you sent me."

43When he had said this, Jesus called in a loud voice, "Lazarus, come out!" 44The dead man came out, his hands and feet wrapped with strips of linen, and a cloth around his face.
Jesus said to them, "Take off the grave clothes and let him go."

1. Why did Jesus weep if he knew he was going to raise Lazarus?

2. Does Jesus pray so that others will hear him pray? Isn't this what he told us not to do (see Matthew 6:5)?

3. Why did Jesus have to tell them to take the grave clothes off Lazarus?

DAY FOUR READING AND QUESTIONS:

45Therefore many of the Jews who had come to visit Mary, and had seen what Jesus did, put their faith in him. 46But some of them went to the Pharisees and told them what Jesus had done. 47Then the chief priests and the Pharisees called a meeting of the Sanhedrin.

"What are we accomplishing?" they asked. "Here is this man performing many miraculous signs. [48]If we let him go on like this, everyone will believe in him, and then the Romans will come and take away both our place and our nation."

[49]Then one of them, named Caiaphas, who was high priest that year, spoke up, "You know nothing at all! [50]You do not realize that it is better for you that one man die for the people than that the whole nation perish."

[51]He did not say this on his own, but as high priest that year he prophesied that Jesus would die for the Jewish nation, [52]and not only for that nation but also for the scattered children of God, to bring them together and make them one. [53]So from that day on they plotted to take his life.

[54]Therefore Jesus no longer moved about publicly among the Jews. Instead he withdrew to a region near the desert, to a village called Ephraim, where he stayed with his disciples.

[55]When it was almost time for the Jewish Passover, many went up from the country to Jerusalem for their ceremonial cleansing before the Passover. [56]They kept looking for Jesus, and as they stood in the temple area they asked one another, "What do you think? Isn't he coming to the Feast at all?" [57]But the chief priests and Pharisees had given orders that if anyone found out where Jesus was, he should report it so that they might arrest him.

1. *What were the Sanhedrin afraid of?*

2. *What did Caiaphas mean when he said it was better for Jesus to die than for the entire nation to perish? What was the deeper meaning of his words?*

3. *Why should an act of mercy, raising the dead, cause the Sanhedrin to plot the death of Jesus? Are good deeds often rewarded with persecution? Why?*

Day Five Reading and Questions:

Go back and read the entire passage.

1. Why didn't Jesus raise more people from the dead? Did he not care about them? Did he not care about those they left behind?

2. Is death the worst thing that can happen to someone?

3. Is Jesus the resurrection and the life only at the last day (as Martha said)? Or is he now the resurrection and the life? How?

MEDITATION ON JOHN 11:1-57

As I write this I have a friend who is dying.

There are things worse than death. However, that is easy to say if you are not the one dying. Or if the one dying is your brother and friend.

Jesus let Lazarus die. That is obvious to Mary and Martha. "Lord, if you had been here, my brother would not have died." It is also obvious to the crowd. "Could not he who opened the eyes of the blind man have kept this man from dying?"

Jesus let Lazarus die. Why? Why if he loved him as a friend?

The obvious answer is that Jesus knew he would raise Lazarus from the dead. But if he knew, why did he weep? Why weep at a tomb that will soon be empty?

We should ask ourselves the same question. Don't we believe that Jesus will raise our loved ones from the dead? Do we not cry at graves that one day will be empty? Why?

One answer is that we miss them. Even knowing I will see them again someday, I still miss my mother, my friends, and my unborn child who have died.

But Jesus did not miss Lazarus. He was about to see him again. Why did he cry?

Because death is not the way things are supposed to be. God made us for life. That's why he put the tree of life in the garden. Jesus is life, life for all who will receive it. There's something not right about death. So Jesus weeps. And so do we.

Yet that weeping turns to joy. Lazarus comes out of the tomb! Our loved ones will also rise. Like Martha, we confess, "I know he will rise again in the resurrection at the last day." But also, like Martha, we may miss the one who right now is resurrection and life.

To miss him is worse than death.

"Teacher, Master, Jesus, may we live in hope and trust this day, knowing that you are the resurrection and the life. May we know that nothing, not even death, can separate us from your love."

BELIEF AND UNBELIEF

(John 12:1-50)

Day One Reading and Questions:

¹Six days before the Passover, Jesus arrived at Bethany, where Lazarus lived, whom Jesus had raised from the dead. ²Here a dinner was given in Jesus' honor. Martha served, while Lazarus was among those reclining at the table with him. ³Then Mary took about a pint of pure nard, an expensive perfume; she poured it on Jesus' feet and wiped his feet with her hair. And the house was filled with the fragrance of the perfume.

⁴But one of his disciples, Judas Iscariot, who was later to betray him, objected, ⁵"Why wasn't this perfume sold and the money given to the poor? It was worth a year's wages." ⁶He did not say this because he cared about the poor but because he was a thief; as keeper of the money bag, he used to help himself to what was put into it.

⁷"Leave her alone," Jesus replied. "It was intended that she should save this perfume for the day of my burial. ⁸You will always have the poor among you, but you will not always have me."

⁹Meanwhile a large crowd of Jews found out that Jesus was there and came, not only because of him but also to see Lazarus, whom he had raised from the dead. ¹⁰So the chief priests made plans to kill

Lazarus as well, [11]for on account of him many of the Jews were going over to Jesus and putting their faith in him.

1. *Why is Mary so extravagant with her gift to Jesus?*

2. *Isn't Judas right to object to such a waste of money? Do we ever object to wasting money at church? How is this different?*

3. *When Jesus says, "You will always have the poor among you," is he telling us not to worry about wasting money on our friends instead of giving to the poor? What does he mean?*

Day Two Reading and Questions:

[12]The next day the great crowd that had come for the Feast heard that Jesus was on his way to Jerusalem. [13]They took palm branches and went out to meet him, shouting,

"Hosanna!"

"Blessed is he who comes in the name of the Lord!"

"Blessed is the King of Israel!"

[14]Jesus found a young donkey and sat upon it, as it is written,

[15]"Do not be afraid, O Daughter of Zion;

see, your king is coming,

seated on a donkey's colt."

[16]At first his disciples did not understand all this. Only after Jesus was glorified did they realize that these things had been written about him and that they had done these things to him.

[17]Now the crowd that was with him when he called Lazarus from the tomb and raised him from the dead continued to spread the word. [18]Many people, because they had heard that he had given this miraculous sign, went out to meet him. [19]So the Pharisees said to one

another, "See, this is getting us nowhere. Look how the whole world has gone after him!"

1. *What did the crowd think of Jesus? Why?*

2. *Why is it significant that Jesus rode into Jerusalem on a donkey?*

3. *Why didn't the disciples understand what was happening at the time?*

Day Three Reading and Questions:

20Now there were some Greeks among those who went up to worship at the Feast. 21They came to Philip, who was from Bethsaida in Galilee, with a request. "Sir," they said, "we would like to see Jesus." 22Philip went to tell Andrew; Andrew and Philip in turn told Jesus.

23Jesus replied, "The hour has come for the Son of Man to be glorified. 24I tell you the truth, unless a kernel of wheat falls to the ground and dies, it remains only a single seed. But if it dies, it produces many seeds. 25The man who loves his life will lose it, while the man who hates his life in this world will keep it for eternal life. 26Whoever serves me must follow me; and where I am, my servant also will be. My Father will honor the one who serves me.

27"Now my heart is troubled, and what shall I say? 'Father, save me from this hour'? No, it was for this very reason I came to this hour. 28Father, glorify your name!"

Then a voice came from heaven, "I have glorified it, and will glorify it again." 29The crowd that was there and heard it said it had thundered; others said an angel had spoken to him.

30Jesus said, "This voice was for your benefit, not mine. 31Now is the time for judgment on this world; now the prince of this world will be driven out. [32]But I, when I am lifted up from the earth, will draw all men to myself." [33]He said this to show the kind of death he was going to die.

[34]The crowd spoke up, "We have heard from the Law that the Christ will remain forever, so how can you say, 'The Son of Man must be lifted up'? Who is this 'Son of Man'?"

[35]Then Jesus told them, "You are going to have the light just a little while longer. Walk while you have the light, before darkness overtakes you. The man who walks in the dark does not know where he is going. [36]Put your trust in the light while you have it, so that you may become sons of light." When he had finished speaking, Jesus left and hid himself from them.

1. *What is the connection between Greeks wanting to see Jesus and the conviction Jesus had that his hour had come?*

2. *Why is Jesus troubled in heart? Was this a lack of courage or faith on his part? Why did Jesus later hide himself?*

3. *What does it mean for the Son of Man to be lifted up? How will this draw all to him?*

DAY FOUR READING AND QUESTIONS:

[37]Even after Jesus had done all these miraculous signs in their presence, they still would not believe in him. [38]This was to fulfill the word of Isaiah the prophet:

"Lord, who has believed our message
and to whom has the arm of the Lord been revealed?"

[39]For this reason they could not believe, because, as Isaiah says elsewhere:

[40]"He has blinded their eyes

and deadened their hearts,

so they can neither see with their eyes,

nor understand with their hearts,

nor turn—and I would heal them."

[41]Isaiah said this because he saw Jesus' glory and spoke about him.

[42]Yet at the same time many even among the leaders believed in him. But because of the Pharisees they would not confess their faith for fear they would be put out of the synagogue; [43]for they loved praise from men more than praise from God.

[44]Then Jesus cried out, "When a man believes in me, he does not believe in me only, but in the one who sent me. [45]When he looks at me, he sees the one who sent me. [46]I have come into the world as a light, so that no one who believes in me should stay in darkness.

[47]"As for the person who hears my words but does not keep them, I do not judge him. For I did not come to judge the world, but to save it. [48]There is a judge for the one who rejects me and does not accept my words; that very word which I spoke will condemn him at the last day. [49]For I did not speak of my own accord, but the Father who sent me commanded me what to say and how to say it. [50]I know that his command leads to eternal life. So whatever I say is just what the Father has told me to say."

1. *If God blinds the hearts of some so they cannot believe, are they still responsible for their unbelief? Why did so many not believe in Jesus?*

2. *Some believed but kept their faith hidden. Why? If one believes but will not confess Jesus, is that genuine faith? What is faith?*

3. *How will the word of Jesus condemn some?*

DAY FIVE READING AND QUESTIONS:

Go back and read the entire passage.

1. How did some show faith in Jesus in this passage? How did some show their lack of faith?

2. What does Jesus do in this passage to draw people to him? What does he say he will do?

3. What is the relationship between Jesus and God the Father in this passage?

MEDITATION ON JOHN 12:1-50

Why believe in Jesus?

Because he's done great things for you. He's raised your brother from the dead. That's why Martha serves him a meal. That's why Mary spends a year's salary on perfume for his feet.

Why believe in Jesus?

Because you expect great things from him. He will make your nation, Israel, great again. He comes as a king, as the savior from the Romans. He brings freedom and prosperity. That's why the crowd greets him with palm branches and shouts.

Why believe in Jesus?

Jesus says to believe because of his words. Because he speaks from God. Because you crave the light. Because he will be lifted up on a cross to die.

Why do some not believe in Jesus?

Because they do not yet know him. Greeks, outsiders to Israel, want to see and know him.

Why do some not believe in Jesus?

Because Jesus does not do what he is expected to do. He allows Mary to waste expensive perfume on him instead of giving the money to the poor.

Why do some not believe in Jesus?

Because of jealousy. The whole world goes to him instead of coming to us, the Pharisees who alone keep the law.

Why do some not believe in Jesus?

Because of fear. Fear that confessing faith in Jesus will cost them their place in the synagogue and in society.

Why do we sometimes not believe in Jesus?

Because God has blinded our eyes and hardened our hearts. The light of Jesus just makes some blind. The words of Jesus can make hearts hard.

Why do we believe in Jesus? Because he's done so much for us? Because we think he will do more? Or because we are willing to be lifted up on the cross with him?

"Father God, open our eyes to see Jesus, the light. Soften our hearts to accept his words as your words. May we always be drawn to his cross."

SERVICE AND LOVE

(John 13:1-14:7)

Day One Reading and Questions:

¹It was just before the Passover Feast. Jesus knew that the time had come for him to leave this world and go to the Father. Having loved his own who were in the world, he now showed them the full extent of his love.

²The evening meal was being served, and the devil had already prompted Judas Iscariot, son of Simon, to betray Jesus. ³Jesus knew that the Father had put all things under his power, and that he had come from God and was returning to God; ⁴so he got up from the meal, took off his outer clothing, and wrapped a towel around his waist. ⁵After that, he poured water into a basin and began to wash his disciples' feet, drying them with the towel that was wrapped around him.

⁶He came to Simon Peter, who said to him, "Lord, are you going to wash my feet?"

⁷Jesus replied, "You do not realize now what I am doing, but later you will understand."

⁸"No," said Peter, "you shall never wash my feet."
Jesus answered, "Unless I wash you, you have no part with me."

⁹"Then, Lord," Simon Peter replied, "not just my feet but my hands and my head as well!"

[10]Jesus answered, "A person who has had a bath needs only to wash his feet; his whole body is clean. And you are clean, though not every one of you." [11]For he knew who was going to betray him, and that was why he said not every one was clean.

[12]When he had finished washing their feet, he put on his clothes and returned to his place. "Do you understand what I have done for you?" he asked them. [13]"You call me 'Teacher' and 'Lord,' and rightly so, for that is what I am. [14]Now that I, your Lord and Teacher, have washed your feet, you also should wash one another's feet. [15]I have set you an example that you should do as I have done for you. [16]I tell you the truth, no servant is greater than his master, nor is a messenger greater than the one who sent him. [17]Now that you know these things, you will be blessed if you do them.

1. *How do Jesus' actions show the full extent of his love? Why is it important that Jesus knew who he was as he washed the disciples' feet?*

2. *Why does Peter not want Jesus to wash his feet?*

3. *Does Jesus want us to literally wash one another's feet? If not, what does he want?*

Day Two Reading and Questions:

[18]"I am not referring to all of you; I know those I have chosen. But this is to fulfill the scripture: 'He who shares my bread has lifted up his heel against me.'

[19]"I am telling you now before it happens, so that when it does happen you will believe that I am He. [20]I tell you the truth, whoever

accepts anyone I send accepts me; and whoever accepts me accepts the one who sent me."

21After he had said this, Jesus was troubled in spirit and testified, "I tell you the truth, one of you is going to betray me."

22His disciples stared at one another, at a loss to know which of them he meant. 23One of them, the disciple whom Jesus loved, was reclining next to him. 24Simon Peter motioned to this disciple and said, "Ask him which one he means."

25Leaning back against Jesus, he asked him, "Lord, who is it?"

26Jesus answered, "It is the one to whom I will give this piece of bread when I have dipped it in the dish." Then, dipping the piece of bread, he gave it to Judas Iscariot, son of Simon. 27As soon as Judas took the bread, Satan entered into him.

"What you are about to do, do quickly," Jesus told him, 28but no one at the meal understood why Jesus said this to him. 29Since Judas had charge of the money, some thought Jesus was telling him to buy what was needed for the Feast, or to give something to the poor. 30As soon as Judas had taken the bread, he went out. And it was night.

1. *This is the first mention of "the disciple whom Jesus loved." What does this mean? Did Jesus not love all the disciples? Does this make Jesus prejudiced or unfair?*

2. *Satan entered Judas. Does this mean Judas is not to blame for his betrayal of Jesus? What does it mean?*

3. *Do you find it strange that none of the disciples understood when Jesus gave the bread to Judas? Why didn't they? What does that say about the behavior of Judas up to this point?*

DAY THREE READING AND QUESTIONS:

³¹When he was gone, Jesus said, "Now is the Son of Man glorified and God is glorified in him. ³²If God is glorified in him, God will glorify the Son in himself, and will glorify him at once.

³³"My children, I will be with you only a little longer. You will look for me, and just as I told the Jews, so I tell you now: Where I am going, you cannot come.

³⁴"A new command I give you: Love one another. As I have loved you, so you must love one another. ³⁵By this all men will know that you are my disciples, if you love one another."

³⁶Simon Peter asked him, "Lord, where are you going?"
Jesus replied, "Where I am going, you cannot follow now, but you will follow later."

³⁷Peter asked, "Lord, why can't I follow you now? I will lay down my life for you."

³⁸Then Jesus answered, "Will you really lay down your life for me? I tell you the truth, before the rooster crows, you will disown me three times!

1. What does "glorified" mean? How will the Son glorify the Father? How will the Father glorify the Son?

2. How is "love one another" a new command? Had not Jesus already told them to love one another? Didn't they already love each other?

3. Does Peter mean it when he offers to lay down his life for Jesus? If he didn't mean it, why did he say it?

Day Four Reading and Questions:

[1]"Do not let your hearts be troubled. Trust in God; trust also in me. [2]In my Father's house are many rooms; if it were not so, I would have told you. I am going there to prepare a place for you. [3]And if I go and prepare a place for you, I will come back and take you to be with me that you also may be where I am. [4]You know the way to the place where I am going."

[5]Thomas said to him, "Lord, we don't know where you are going, so how can we know the way?"

[6]Jesus answered, "I am the way and the truth and the life. No one comes to the Father except through me. [7]If you really knew me, you would know my Father as well. From now on, you do know him and have seen him."

1. *What is the Father's house? How does Jesus prepare a place for us there?*

2. *Do we know the way to the Father's house? Why (like Thomas) might we think we do not know the way?*

3. *How is Jesus the way?*

Day Five Reading and Questions:

Go back and read the entire passage.

1. *How does washing feet relate to the new command?*

2. *How does Jesus being glorified relate to the cross?*

3. How does following Jesus as the way to the Father require trust?

MEDITATION ON JOHN 13:1-14:7

Have you ever been to a foot washing?

I've only been once in my life. I know for many Christians this is a regular practice, but for me, it was strange.

I think I understand Peter. I had no trouble washing another's feet. In a strange way, I even felt honored to serve him as Jesus did. But I didn't want my feet washed. I have ugly feet. Discolored toes. I'd rather wash my own feet, thank you. For me, submitting to foot washing was a wonderfully humbling experience.

I know the point here is that we should serve others instead of being served. But I wonder if I am not the only one like Peter. In order to learn the lesson of service, we must first learn to let Jesus serve us. He goes to prepare a place for us. We dare not think we must prepare our own place by the service we do. He calls us to be glorified with him. We must follow him as the way, knowing that the way to glory is always the way of service.

It is easy to intend to serve. It is easy to pledge loyalty, even in the face of death. It is much harder to open our eyes to see opportunities to serve. Much harder to actually face death (just ask Peter).

Loving one another is not about good intentions or pious pledges. It is all about ordinary days and ordinary ways of serving others. That is the way of Jesus.

"Lord Jesus, you have washed and cleansed us. This day open our eyes to opportunities to serve as you have served."

SPIRIT AND VINE

(John 14:8-15:27)

DAY ONE READING AND QUESTIONS:

[8]Philip said, "Lord, show us the Father and that will be enough for us."

[9]Jesus answered: "Don't you know me, Philip, even after I have been among you such a long time? Anyone who has seen me has seen the Father. How can you say, 'Show us the Father'? [10]Don't you believe that I am in the Father, and that the Father is in me? The words I say to you are not just my own. Rather, it is the Father, living in me, who is doing his work. [11]Believe me when I say that I am in the Father and the Father is in me; or at least believe on the evidence of the miracles themselves. [12]I tell you the truth, anyone who has faith in me will do what I have been doing. He will do even greater things than these, because I am going to the Father. [13]And I will do whatever you ask in my name, so that the Son may bring glory to the Father. [14]You may ask me for anything in my name, and I will do it.

[15]"If you love me, you will obey what I command. [16]And I will ask the Father, and he will give you another Counselor to be with you forever— [17]the Spirit of truth. The world cannot accept him, because it neither sees him nor knows him. But you know him, for he lives with you and will be in you. [18]I will not leave you as orphans; I will

come to you. [19]Before long, the world will not see me anymore, but you will see me. Because I live, you also will live. [20]On that day you will realize that I am in my Father, and you are in me, and I am in you. [21]Whoever has my commands and obeys them, he is the one who loves me. He who loves me will be loved by my Father, and I too will love him and show myself to him."

1. *Jesus says those who have faith in him will do greater works than he did. How can this be true? Can we do more than Jesus?*

2. *The Holy Spirit is here called a Counselor. Other versions translate this word Comforter, Helper, or Advocate. How is the Holy Spirit each of these four?*

3. *Jesus says he will not leave us as orphans. How is Jesus still with (and in) his disciples after his ascension?*

Day Two Reading and Questions:

[22]Then Judas (not Judas Iscariot) said, "But, Lord, why do you intend to show yourself to us and not to the world?"

[23]Jesus replied, "If anyone loves me, he will obey my teaching. My Father will love him, and we will come to him and make our home with him. [24]He who does not love me will not obey my teaching. These words you hear are not my own; they belong to the Father who sent me.

[25]"All this I have spoken while still with you. [26]But the Counselor, the Holy Spirit, whom the Father will send in my name, will teach you all things and will remind you of everything I have said to you. [27]Peace I leave with you; my peace I give you. I do not give to you as the world gives. Do not let your hearts be troubled and do not be afraid.

²⁸"You heard me say, 'I am going away and I am coming back to you.' If you loved me, you would be glad that I am going to the Father, for the Father is greater than I. ²⁹I have told you now before it happens, so that when it does happen you will believe. ³⁰I will not speak with you much longer, for the prince of this world is coming. He has no hold on me, ³¹but the world must learn that I love the Father and that I do exactly what my Father has commanded me. "Come now; let us leave.

1. How do the Father and Jesus make their home with us?

2. What kind of peace does Jesus give? How is it different from the world's peace?

3. Who is the prince of this world? How was he coming to Jesus?

Day Three Reading and Questions:

¹"I am the true vine, and my Father is the gardener. ²He cuts off every branch in me that bears no fruit, while every branch that does bear fruit he prunes so that it will be even more fruitful. ³You are already clean because of the word I have spoken to you. ⁴Remain in me, and I will remain in you. No branch can bear fruit by itself; it must remain in the vine. Neither can you bear fruit unless you remain in me.

⁵"I am the vine; you are the branches. If a man remains in me and I in him, he will bear much fruit; apart from me you can do nothing. ⁶If anyone does not remain in me, he is like a branch that is thrown away and withers; such branches are picked up, thrown into the fire and burned. ⁷If you remain in me and my words remain in you, ask whatever you wish, and it will be given you. ⁸This is to my Father's glory, that you bear much fruit, showing yourselves to be my disciples.

⁹"As the Father has loved me, so have I loved you. Now remain in my love. ¹⁰If you obey my commands, you will remain in my love, just as I have obeyed my Father's commands and remain in his love. ¹¹I have told you this so that my joy may be in you and that your joy may be complete. ¹²My command is this: Love each other as I have loved you. ¹³Greater love has no one than this, that he lay down his life for his friends. ¹⁴You are my friends if you do what I command. ¹⁵I no longer call you servants, because a servant does not know his master's business. Instead, I have called you friends, for everything that I learned from my Father I have made known to you. ¹⁶You did not choose me, but I chose you and appointed you to go and bear fruit—fruit that will last. Then the Father will give you whatever you ask in my name. ¹⁷This is my command: Love each other.

1. How do we remain in Jesus as the vine? What remains in us? What else do we remain in?

2. What will Jesus do for us if we remain in him?

3. What does it mean to be friends of Jesus?

DAY FOUR READING AND QUESTIONS:

¹⁸"If the world hates you, keep in mind that it hated me first. ¹⁹If you belonged to the world, it would love you as its own. As it is, you do not belong to the world, but I have chosen you out of the world. That is why the world hates you. ²⁰Remember the words I spoke to you: 'No servant is greater than his master.' If they persecuted me, they will persecute you also. If they obeyed my teaching, they will obey yours also. ²¹They will treat you this way because of my name, for they do not know the One who sent me. ²²If I had not come and

spoken to them, they would not be guilty of sin. Now, however, they have no excuse for their sin. [23]He who hates me hates my Father as well. [24]If I had not done among them what no one else did, they would not be guilty of sin. But now they have seen these miracles, and yet they have hated both me and my Father. [25]But this is to fulfill what is written in their Law: 'They hated me without reason.'

[26]"When the Counselor comes, whom I will send to you from the Father, the Spirit of truth who goes out from the Father, he will testify about me. [27]And you also must testify, for you have been with me from the beginning.

1. *Why does the world hate the followers of Jesus? Are we hated by the world today? Do you feel that way?*

2. *Why is there no excuse for not believing in Jesus?*

3. *Are we to testify about Jesus today? What does that look like?*

DAY FIVE READING AND QUESTIONS:

Go back and read the entire passage.

1. *Who are we to love in this passage?*

2. *What is the role of the Holy Spirit in this passage?*

3. *What fruit are we to bear for Jesus? How can we be fruitful?*

MEDITATION ON JOHN 14:8-15:27

Show me.

Show me the Father. Just a glimpse of God, that's all we ask for. Why doesn't he show himself clearly to everyone?

But he does. "Anyone who has seen me has seen the Father."

Live in me. Isn't that what we want God to do? Or is that too intimate? Too personal? Too frightening? Yet that is precisely what Jesus promises. The Spirit "lives with you and will be in you."

Give me peace. Isn't that what we long for? A deep, abiding peace that no trouble can touch. "Peace I leave with you; my peace I give you."

Use me. Jesus promises to make us useful. We will bear fruit, abundant clusters of grapes, if only we remain in the vine. We will testify because the Spirit of truth is in us.

Be my friend. Jesus is. What's more, he calls us his friends. Friends of Jesus. Friends of God.

The promises Jesus gives are overwhelming. Peace. Love. Friendship. Purpose. He shows us God himself.

How can we respond to such overwhelming promises, except in faith and love?

"Friend Jesus, you give us peace, purpose, and love. This day may we remain in you as you remain in us through your Holy Spirit."

TROUBLE AND PRAYER

(John 16:1-17:26)

Day One Reading and Questions:

¹"All this I have told you so that you will not go astray. ²They will put you out of the synagogue; in fact, a time is coming when anyone who kills you will think he is offering a service to God. ³They will do such things because they have not known the Father or me. ⁴I have told you this, so that when the time comes you will remember that I warned you. I did not tell you this at first because I was with you.

⁵"Now I am going to him who sent me, yet none of you asks me, 'Where are you going?' ⁶Because I have said these things, you are filled with grief. ⁷But I tell you the truth: It is for your good that I am going away. Unless I go away, the Counselor will not come to you; but if I go, I will send him to you. ⁸When he comes, he will convict the world of guilt in regard to sin and righteousness and judgment: ⁹in regard to sin, because men do not believe in me; ¹⁰in regard to righteousness, because I am going to the Father, where you can see me no longer; ¹¹and in regard to judgment, because the prince of this world now stands condemned.

¹²"I have much more to say to you, more than you can now bear. ¹³But when he, the Spirit of truth, comes, he will guide you into all truth. He will not speak on his own; he will speak only what he hears,

and he will tell you what is yet to come. ¹⁴He will bring glory to me by taking from what is mine and making it known to you. ¹⁵All that belongs to the Father is mine. That is why I said the Spirit will take from what is mine and make it known to you.

> 1. *How is it helpful to know that some will oppose us because we follow Jesus?*

> 2. *How was it good for those disciples that Jesus was going away? How is it good for us?*

> 3. *What does the Spirit do in this passage?*

Day Two Reading and Questions:

¹⁶"In a little while you will see me no more, and then after a little while you will see me."

¹⁷Some of his disciples said to one another, "What does he mean by saying, 'In a little while you will see me no more, and then after a little while you will see me,' and 'Because I am going to the Father'?" ¹⁸They kept asking, "What does he mean by 'a little while'? We don't understand what he is saying."

¹⁹Jesus saw that they wanted to ask him about this, so he said to them, "Are you asking one another what I meant when I said, 'In a little while you will see me no more, and then after a little while you will see me'? ²⁰I tell you the truth, you will weep and mourn while the world rejoices. You will grieve, but your grief will turn to joy. ²¹A woman giving birth to a child has pain because her time has come; but when her baby is born she forgets the anguish because of her joy that a child is born into the world. ²²So with you: Now is your time of grief, but I will see you again and you will rejoice, and no one will take

away your joy. [23]In that day you will no longer ask me anything. I tell you the truth, my Father will give you whatever you ask in my name. [24]Until now you have not asked for anything in my name. Ask and you will receive, and your joy will be complete.

[25]"Though I have been speaking figuratively, a time is coming when I will no longer use this kind of language but will tell you plainly about my Father. [26]In that day you will ask in my name. I am not saying that I will ask the Father on your behalf. [27]No, the Father himself loves you because you have loved me and have believed that I came from God. [28]I came from the Father and entered the world; now I am leaving the world and going back to the Father."

[29]Then Jesus' disciples said, "Now you are speaking clearly and without figures of speech. [30]Now we can see that you know all things and that you do not even need to have anyone ask you questions. This makes us believe that you came from God."

[31]"You believe at last!" Jesus answered. [32]"But a time is coming, and has come, when you will be scattered, each to his own home. You will leave me all alone. Yet I am not alone, for my Father is with me.

[33]"I have told you these things, so that in me you may have peace. In this world you will have trouble. But take heart! I have overcome the world."

1. *Why do you think the disciples did not understand Jesus? Should they have understood?*

2. *When will the disciples grieve? When will their grief be turned to joy?*

3. *What does it mean to ask in the name of Jesus? Is this more than ending our prayers, "in Jesus' name"?*

Day Three Reading and Questions:

[1]After Jesus said this, he looked toward heaven and prayed:

"Father, the time has come. Glorify your Son, that your Son may glorify you. [2]For you granted him authority over all people that he might give eternal life to all those you have given him. [3]Now this is eternal life: that they may know you, the only true God, and Jesus Christ, whom you have sent. [4]I have brought you glory on earth by completing the work you gave me to do. [5]And now, Father, glorify me in your presence with the glory I had with you before the world began.

[6]"I have revealed you to those whom you gave me out of the world. They were yours; you gave them to me and they have obeyed your word. [7]Now they know that everything you have given me comes from you. [8]For I gave them the words you gave me and they accepted them. They knew with certainty that I came from you, and they believed that you sent me. [9]I pray for them. I am not praying for the world, but for those you have given me, for they are yours. [10]All I have is yours, and all you have is mine. And glory has come to me through them. [11]I will remain in the world no longer, but they are still in the world, and I am coming to you. Holy Father, protect them by the power of your name—the name you gave me—so that they may be one as we are one. [12]While I was with them, I protected them and kept them safe by that name you gave me. None has been lost except the one doomed to destruction so that Scripture would be fulfilled.

[13]"I am coming to you now, but I say these things while I am still in the world, so that they may have the full measure of my joy within them. [14]I have given them your word and the world has hated them, for they are not of the world any more than I am of the world. [15]My prayer is not that you take them out of the world but that you protect them from the evil one. [16]They are not of the world, even as I am not of it. [17]Sanctify them by the truth; your word is truth. [18]As you sent

me into the world, I have sent them into the world. ¹⁹For them I sanctify myself, that they too may be truly sanctified.

1. In this prayer Jesus prays for glory. What does glory mean? Is it right for us to pray that God would glorify us? If so, how does he do so?

2. What does Jesus pray for concerning his disciples?

3. What does it mean to be sanctified? How are we sanctified?

Day Four Reading and Questions:

²⁰"My prayer is not for them alone. I pray also for those who will believe in me through their message, ²¹that all of them may be one, Father, just as you are in me and I am in you. May they also be in us so that the world may believe that you have sent me. ²²I have given them the glory that you gave me, that they may be one as we are one: ²³I in them and you in me. May they be brought to complete unity to let the world know that you sent me and have loved them even as you have loved me.

²⁴"Father, I want those you have given me to be with me where I am, and to see my glory, the glory you have given me because you loved me before the creation of the world.

²⁵"Righteous Father, though the world does not know you, I know you, and they know that you have sent me. ²⁶I have made you known to them, and will continue to make you known in order that the love you have for me may be in them and that I myself may be in them."

1. Did Jesus pray for us the night he was betrayed? How does this make you feel?

2. Why is Christian unity important? What is the purpose of Christian unity?

3. How does Jesus continue to make God known to us?

Day Five Reading and Questions:

Go back and read the entire passage.

1. What connection do you see between what Jesus says about the Holy Spirit and how Jesus prays?

2. What do you find striking and unusual about this prayer? What would you expect Jesus to pray about as he faces the cross? Is this prayer a model for us? Why or why not?

3. What is the relationship between Jesus and the Father expressed in this prayer? Between Jesus and his disciples? Between Jesus and us?

MEDITATION ON JOHN 16:1-17:26

It's dangerous to follow Jesus. If we are true disciples, even some religious people will turn against us, throw us out of church, and think they are serving God by doing it. Following Jesus means trouble. That trouble and danger might scare us into leaving Jesus, of going astray. One great danger is that we will turn against each other and divide the body of Christ. Yet Jesus wants his followers to be one.

What do we need to remain faithful?

We need help. Jesus gives us a Helper, a Counselor, the Spirit of truth who allows us to see through the world's illusions and to focus on Jesus, the truth. There is no greater comfort than to know that God the Father and Jesus himself make their home with us through the Holy Spirit within.

We need prayer. Jesus assures us that anything we ask in his name the Father will do for us. And what would we ask but to be strong and faithful? In that we have complete joy.

But Jesus does more than tell us to pray. He prays for us. He prays for our safety. He prays for our joy. He prays for our sanctification. Here, on the very night he will face betrayal and suffering, he prays not only for his own glory but for ours. That glory comes only as we follow Jesus to the cross. It comes only after faithfulness in the face of opposition.

What's more, Jesus prays that all who believe in him will share in the unity of the Father and the Son. Christian division is a deep scandal that keeps the world from believing. There is no easy way to heal the divisions among us. But there is a first step. Like Jesus, we must pray that God make us one. And if we pray for it, we must be willing for God to answer through us. We must make every effort to be one in the Spirit.

What does it take to be faithful? It takes love. Love from the Father. Love from the Son. Love for one another. It is that love that Christians show when they are one.

"Loving Father, make us one in Christ. Fill us with your love, even for those who oppose you and us. Protect us. Glorify us. Make us holy."

CONFIDENCE AND BETRAYAL

(John 18:1-40)

Day One Reading and Questions:

¹When he had finished praying, Jesus left with his disciples and crossed the Kidron Valley. On the other side there was an olive grove, and he and his disciples went into it.

²Now Judas, who betrayed him, knew the place, because Jesus had often met there with his disciples. ³So Judas came to the grove, guiding a detachment of soldiers and some officials from the chief priests and Pharisees. They were carrying torches, lanterns and weapons.

⁴Jesus, knowing all that was going to happen to him, went out and asked them, "Who is it you want?"

⁵"Jesus of Nazareth," they replied.

"I am he," Jesus said. (And Judas the traitor was standing there with them.) ⁶When Jesus said, "I am he," they drew back and fell to the ground.

⁷Again he asked them, "Who is it you want?"
And they said, "Jesus of Nazareth."

⁸"I told you that I am he," Jesus answered. "If you are looking for me, then let these men go." ⁹This happened so that the words he had spoken would be fulfilled: "I have not lost one of those you gave me."

[10]Then Simon Peter, who had a sword, drew it and struck the high priest's servant, cutting off his right ear. (The servant's name was Malchus.)

[11]Jesus commanded Peter, "Put your sword away! Shall I not drink the cup the Father has given me?"

1. How does Jesus show that he is in control of the events in the garden?

2. Why did the soldiers fall to the ground when Jesus spoke?

3. Why does Jesus tell Peter to put his sword away?

DAY TWO READING AND QUESTIONS:

[12]Then the detachment of soldiers with its commander and the Jewish officials arrested Jesus. They bound him [13]and brought him first to Annas, who was the father-in-law of Caiaphas, the high priest that year. [14]Caiaphas was the one who had advised the Jews that it would be good if one man died for the people.

[15]Simon Peter and another disciple were following Jesus. Because this disciple was known to the high priest, he went with Jesus into the high priest's courtyard, [16]but Peter had to wait outside at the door. The other disciple, who was known to the high priest, came back, spoke to the girl on duty there and brought Peter in.

[17]"You are not one of his disciples, are you?" the girl at the door asked Peter.

He replied, "I am not."

[18]It was cold, and the servants and officials stood around a fire they had made to keep warm. Peter also was standing with them, warming himself.

[19]Meanwhile, the high priest questioned Jesus about his disciples and his teaching.

[20]"I have spoken openly to the world," Jesus replied. "I always taught in synagogues or at the temple, where all the Jews come together. I said nothing in secret. [21]Why question me? Ask those who heard me. Surely they know what I said."

[22]When Jesus said this, one of the officials nearby struck him in the face. "Is this the way you answer the high priest?" he demanded.

[23]"If I said something wrong," Jesus replied, "testify as to what is wrong. But if I spoke the truth, why did you strike me?" [24]Then Annas sent him, still bound, to Caiaphas the high priest.

1. *Why would the girl at the door think Peter was a disciple? Why did Peter want to go into the courtyard if he was afraid to admit his discipleship?*

2. *Why did Annas question Jesus about his teachings? Didn't the Jewish officials know what Jesus taught?*

3. *Why did the official strike Jesus?*

Day Three Reading and Questions:

[25]As Simon Peter stood warming himself, he was asked, "You are not one of his disciples, are you?"

He denied it, saying, "I am not."

[26]One of the high priest's servants, a relative of the man whose ear Peter had cut off, challenged him, "Didn't I see you with him in the olive grove?" [27]Again Peter denied it, and at that moment a rooster began to crow.

1. Why did Peter deny Jesus?

2. Why is it significant that the man who questions Peter is a relative of the man whose ear he cut off?

3. Is Peter's denial worse than the desertion of the other disciples? Is it as bad as the betrayal of Judas?

DAY FOUR READING AND QUESTIONS:

²⁸Then the Jews led Jesus from Caiaphas to the palace of the Roman governor. By now it was early morning, and to avoid ceremonial uncleanness the Jews did not enter the palace; they wanted to be able to eat the Passover. ²⁹So Pilate came out to them and asked, "What charges are you bringing against this man?"

³⁰"If he were not a criminal," they replied, "we would not have handed him over to you."

³¹Pilate said, "Take him yourselves and judge him by your own law."

"But we have no right to execute anyone," the Jews objected. ³²This happened so that the words Jesus had spoken indicating the kind of death he was going to die would be fulfilled.

³³Pilate then went back inside the palace, summoned Jesus and asked him, "Are you the king of the Jews?"

³⁴"Is that your own idea," Jesus asked, "or did others talk to you about me?"

³⁵"Am I a Jew?" Pilate replied. "It was your people and your chief priests who handed you over to me. What is it you have done?"

³⁶Jesus said, "My kingdom is not of this world. If it were, my servants would fight to prevent my arrest by the Jews. But now my kingdom is from another place."

³⁷"You are a king, then!" said Pilate.

Jesus answered, "You are right in saying I am a king. In fact, for this reason I was born, and for this I came into the world, to testify to the truth. Everyone on the side of truth listens to me."

[38]"What is truth?" Pilate asked. With this he went out again to the Jews and said, "I find no basis for a charge against him. [39]But it is your custom for me to release to you one prisoner at the time of the Passover. Do you want me to release 'the king of the Jews'?"

[40]They shouted back, "No, not him! Give us Barabbas!" Now Barabbas had taken part in a rebellion.

1. Why does Pilate ask Jesus if he is a king? Why doesn't Pilate immediately condemn Jesus when Jesus admits to being a king?

2. Why does Pilate want to release Jesus?

3. What does Pilate's question, "What is truth?" tell you about him?

Day Five Reading and Questions:

Go back and read the entire passage:

1. Does Jesus seem like a helpless victim in this passage? What is the attitude of Jesus here?

2. Contrast the attitude of Peter with that of Jesus in this passage.

3. What attitude does Pilate have toward Jesus?

MEDITATION ON JOHN 18:1-40

Have you ever felt betrayed? Stabbed in the back? Have you ever depended on someone to defend you, only to find they were your accuser?

It's hard being betrayed. Feeling that your best friends have turned against you. When that happens, we react with bewilderment, hurt, and anger.

That's not how Jesus reacts. Oh, no doubt he felt betrayed. Judas turns him over to the authorities. Peter denies him. The high priests, God's anointed, should have recognized and praised Jesus. Instead they condemn him. Pilate, the minister of justice, does not have the courage to do right by Jesus.

Jesus is betrayed by friends, by religious leaders, and by the government. He could have even have thought he was betrayed by his Father. How does he react? With bewilderment? Hurt? Anger?

No. He reacts with absolute confidence. When they come to arrest him, he is so confident that the soldiers jump back in fear. He has to tell them twice who he is! Before the high priests, he speaks the truth so boldly that they hit him in the mouth. Standing before Pilate who can condemn him to a horrible death, Jesus states clearly that he is a king. He speaks truth to Pilate who cannot recognize truth.

This confidence of Jesus is astounding. Having warned his disciples (including us) that they will face persecution, Jesus now shows them (and us) how to face it. Not with fear, anger, or resignation, but with absolute confidence in a God who is in control. If Jesus can face the cross this way, surely through his Holy Spirit we can face whatever comes our way today with boldness.

"Lord Jesus, give us confidence in you and your Spirit, not in ourselves. Stand beside us in boldness this day."

POWER AND FEAR

(John 19:1-42)

DAY ONE READING AND QUESTIONS:

[1] Then Pilate took Jesus and had him flogged. [2] The soldiers twisted together a crown of thorns and put it on his head. They clothed him in a purple robe [3] and went up to him again and again, saying, "Hail, king of the Jews!" And they struck him in the face.

[4] Once more Pilate came out and said to the Jews, "Look, I am bringing him out to you to let you know that I find no basis for a charge against him." [5] When Jesus came out wearing the crown of thorns and the purple robe, Pilate said to them, "Here is the man!"

[6] As soon as the chief priests and their officials saw him, they shouted, "Crucify! Crucify!"

But Pilate answered, "You take him and crucify him. As for me, I find no basis for a charge against him."

[7] The Jews insisted, "We have a law, and according to that law he must die, because he claimed to be the Son of God."

[8] When Pilate heard this, he was even more afraid, [9] and he went back inside the palace. "Where do you come from?" he asked Jesus, but Jesus gave him no answer. [10] "Do you refuse to speak to me?" Pilate said. "Don't you realize I have power either to free you or to crucify you?"

[11]Jesus answered, "You would have no power over me if it were not given to you from above. Therefore the one who handed me over to you is guilty of a greater sin."

[12]From then on, Pilate tried to set Jesus free, but the Jews kept shouting, "If you let this man go, you are no friend of Caesar. Anyone who claims to be a king opposes Caesar."

[13]When Pilate heard this, he brought Jesus out and sat down on the judge's seat at a place known as the Stone Pavement (which in Aramaic is Gabbatha). [14]It was the day of Preparation of Passover Week, about the sixth hour.

"Here is your king," Pilate said to the Jews.

[15]But they shouted, "Take him away! Take him away! Crucify him!"

"Shall I crucify your king?" Pilate asked.

"We have no king but Caesar," the chief priests answered.

1. Why did Pilate have Jesus flogged if he thought he was innocent?

2. Why is Pilate afraid? Does Jesus seem afraid? Should he be?

3. Why is it amazing that the chief priests would say, "We have no king but Caesar"?

Day Two Reading and Questions:

[16]Finally Pilate handed him over to them to be crucified.

So the soldiers took charge of Jesus. [17]Carrying his own cross, he went out to the place of the Skull (which in Aramaic is called Golgotha). [18]Here they crucified him, and with him two others—one on each side and Jesus in the middle.

[19]Pilate had a notice prepared and fastened to the cross. It read: JESUS OF NAZARETH, THE KING OF THE JEWS. [20]Many of the Jews

read this sign, for the place where Jesus was crucified was near the city, and the sign was written in Aramaic, Latin and Greek. [21]The chief priests of the Jews protested to Pilate, "Do not write 'The King of the Jews,' but that this man claimed to be king of the Jews."

[22]Pilate answered, "What I have written, I have written."

[23]When the soldiers crucified Jesus, they took his clothes, dividing them into four shares, one for each of them, with the undergarment remaining. This garment was seamless, woven in one piece from top to bottom.

[24]"Let's not tear it," they said to one another. "Let's decide by lot
who will get it."

This happened that the scripture might be fulfilled which said,
"They divided my garments among them
and cast lots for my clothing."

So this is what the soldiers did.

[25]Near the cross of Jesus stood his mother, his mother's sister, Mary the wife of Clopas, and Mary Magdalene. [26]When Jesus saw his mother there, and the disciple whom he loved standing nearby, he said to his mother, "Dear woman, here is your son," [27]and to the disciple, "Here is your mother." From that time on, this disciple took her into his home.

*1. Why do you think Pilate wrote what he did on the notice on
    the cross?*

*2. What is the significance of the soldiers casting lots for Jesus'
    garment?*

3. What does the story about Mary tell us about Jesus?

Day Three Reading and Questions:

[28]Later, knowing that all was now completed, and so that the Scripture would be fulfilled, Jesus said, "I am thirsty." [29]A jar of wine vinegar was there, so they soaked a sponge in it, put the sponge on a stalk of the hyssop plant, and lifted it to Jesus' lips. [30]When he had received the drink, Jesus said, "It is finished." With that, he bowed his head and gave up his spirit.

[31]Now it was the day of Preparation, and the next day was to be a special Sabbath. Because the Jews did not want the bodies left on the crosses during the Sabbath, they asked Pilate to have the legs broken and the bodies taken down. [32]The soldiers therefore came and broke the legs of the first man who had been crucified with Jesus, and then those of the other. [33]But when they came to Jesus and found that he was already dead, they did not break his legs. [34]Instead, one of the soldiers pierced Jesus' side with a spear, bringing a sudden flow of blood and water. [35]The man who saw it has given testimony, and his testimony is true. He knows that he tells the truth, and he testifies so that you also may believe. [36]These things happened so that the scripture would be fulfilled: "Not one of his bones will be broken," [37]and, as another scripture says, "They will look on the one they have pierced."

1. *What does Jesus mean by "It is finished"?*

2. *Is the writer of John an eyewitness to the crucifixion? Does this make his testimony believable?*

3. *Name all the ways Jesus fulfills scripture in this passage. Why is this significant?*

Day Four Reading and Questions:

[38]Later, Joseph of Arimathea asked Pilate for the body of Jesus. Now Joseph was a disciple of Jesus, but secretly because he feared the Jews. With Pilate's permission, he came and took the body away. [39]He was accompanied by Nicodemus, the man who earlier had visited Jesus at night. Nicodemus brought a mixture of myrrh and aloes, about seventy-five pounds. [40]Taking Jesus' body, the two of them wrapped it, with the spices, in strips of linen. This was in accordance with Jewish burial customs. [41]At the place where Jesus was crucified, there was a garden, and in the garden a new tomb, in which no one had ever been laid. [42]Because it was the Jewish day of Preparation and since the tomb was nearby, they laid Jesus there.

1. *What does it mean to be a secret disciple? Can one be a true disciple and do it secretly?*

2. *Was Nicodemus a secret disciple? Why do you think he came to Jesus by night? Why does he publicly show his faith here?*

3. *Is it important who buried Jesus? Why did these two bury him?*

Day Five Reading and Questions:

Go back and read the entire passage.

1. *Does John tell us much about the agony of Jesus on the cross? Why or why not?*

2. *What seems to concern Jesus most while he is on the cross?*

3. Are there secret disciples today? If so, what does that mean?

MEDITATION ON JOHN 19:1-42

Power. God has the power. He gives it to Jesus.

Power. It's strange to talk about power on the cross. Hanging helpless on a cross seems the very opposite of power. Crucifixion is meant to show how powerful Rome is and how powerless the crucified one is.

But it didn't work that way with Jesus. In his interview (not so much a trial) with Pilate, Jesus tells the representative of the might of Rome that God alone has power and he has given that power to Jesus.

On the cross, it is Jesus who is in control. He carries his own cross. He takes care of his mother. He intentionally fulfills scripture. He does all that God demands and says, "It is finished."

Jesus is not afraid, even on the cross.

By contrast, Pilate is afraid. He's so afraid of the possibility of Jewish rebellion, that he will not set Jesus free, even though he thinks he is innocent. He's afraid of Jesus. Perhaps he is the Son of God. But Pilate has no genuine fear of God. He will not admit who really has the power.

Some of the disciples are afraid. Only one, the one Jesus loves, is at the cross. Other disciples, Joseph and Nicodemus, overcome their fear to bury him. Perhaps they begin to catch a glimpse of Jesus' power even as they lay his body in the tomb.

But the clearest display of power is yet to come.

What about us? Are we fearful disciples? Secret disciples? Afraid and ashamed of the cross? Or can we, by faith, even see power in one who hangs on a tree?

"Almighty Father, all power is yours. Let me this day see your power in Jesus, even in the middle of pain, defeat, and brokenness."

SEEING AND BELEIVING

(John 20:1-29)

DAY ONE READING AND QUESTIONS:

¹Early on the first day of the week, while it was still dark, Mary Magdalene went to the tomb and saw that the stone had been removed from the entrance. ²So she came running to Simon Peter and the other disciple, the one Jesus loved, and said, "They have taken the Lord out of the tomb, and we don't know where they have put him!"

³So Peter and the other disciple started for the tomb. ⁴Both were running, but the other disciple outran Peter and reached the tomb first. ⁵He bent over and looked in at the strips of linen lying there but did not go in. ⁶Then Simon Peter, who was behind him, arrived and went into the tomb. He saw the strips of linen lying there, ⁷as well as the burial cloth that had been around Jesus' head. The cloth was folded up by itself, separate from the linen. ⁸Finally the other disciple, who had reached the tomb first, also went inside. He saw and believed. ⁹(They still did not understand from Scripture that Jesus had to rise from the dead.)

1. Did Mary Magdalene expect Jesus to rise from the dead? Did Peter and the other disciple?

2. Why do you think the other disciple believed in the resurrection?

3. Why didn't they understand from Scripture about the resurrection? Should they have understood? Can one read Scripture and not understand? What brings understanding?

DAY TWO READING AND QUESTIONS:

[10]Then the disciples went back to their homes, [11]but Mary stood outside the tomb crying. As she wept, she bent over to look into the tomb [12]and saw two angels in white, seated where Jesus' body had been, one at the head and the other at the foot.

[13]They asked her, "Woman, why are you crying?"

"They have taken my Lord away," she said, "and I don't know where they have put him." [14]At this, she turned around and saw Jesus standing there, but she did not realize that it was Jesus.

[15]"Woman," he said, "why are you crying? Who is it you are looking for?"

Thinking he was the gardener, she said, "Sir, if you have carried him away, tell me where you have put him, and I will get him."

[16]Jesus said to her, "Mary."

She turned toward him and cried out in Aramaic, "Rabboni!" (which means Teacher).

[17]Jesus said, "Do not hold on to me, for I have not yet returned to the Father. Go instead to my brothers and tell them, 'I am returning to my Father and your Father, to my God and your God.' "

[18]Mary Magdalene went to the disciples with the news: "I have seen the Lord!" And she told them that he had said these things to her.

1. Why is Mary crying? What does this tell you about her view of Jesus?

2. *Why do you think Mary did not recognize Jesus at first? When did she recognize him?*

3. *What did Jesus mean by, "Do not hold on to me, for I have not yet returned to the Father"?*

Day Three Reading and Questions:

[19]On the evening of that first day of the week, when the disciples were together, with the doors locked for fear of the Jews, Jesus came and stood among them and said, "Peace be with you!" [20]After he said this, he showed them his hands and side. The disciples were overjoyed when they saw the Lord.

[21]Again Jesus said, "Peace be with you! As the Father has sent me, I am sending you." [22]And with that he breathed on them and said, "Receive the Holy Spirit. [23]If you forgive anyone his sins, they are forgiven; if you do not forgive them, they are not forgiven."

1. *Jesus says he is sending the disciples. Is this what we usually call the Great Commission? Where is he sending them? What is he sending them to do?*

2. *Why does Jesus give the Holy Spirit at this time? How does he give it? Why is that significant?*

3. *How do the disciples have the power to forgive sins? Does anyone have this power today? Do we?*

Day Four Reading and Questions:

[24]Now Thomas (called Didymus), one of the Twelve, was not with the disciples when Jesus came. [25]So the other disciples told him, "We have seen the Lord!"

But he said to them, "Unless I see the nail marks in his hands and put my finger where the nails were, and put my hand into his side, I will not believe it."

[26]A week later his disciples were in the house again, and Thomas was with them. Though the doors were locked, Jesus came and stood among them and said, "Peace be with you!" [27]Then he said to Thomas, "Put your finger here; see my hands. Reach out your hand and put it into my side. Stop doubting and believe."

[28]Thomas said to him, "My Lord and my God!"

[29]Then Jesus told him, "Because you have seen me, you have believed; blessed are those who have not seen and yet have believed."

1. *Why does Thomas doubt? Would you doubt your friends if they told you someone had been raised from the dead?*

2. *Why are the doors still locked, even after the disciples had seen Jesus? Are they still afraid of the Jewish authorities?*

3. *How can we believe in Jesus if we have never seen him? What makes us believe?*

Day Five Reading and Questions:

Go back and read the entire passage.

1. *Why do you think Jesus first appeared to Mary Magdalene after his resurrection? Why didn't he appear to the disciples first?*

2. *Why does Jesus greet the disciples with "Peace be with you"? Is this more than "hello"? What is the relationship between resurrection and peace?*

3. *Why does Thomas react so strongly to Jesus, calling him, "My Lord and my God"?*

MEDITATION ON JOHN 20:1-29

Out of love for Jesus, Mary Magdalene comes to the tomb. She comes to honor the memory of a dead friend. She does not expect to see Jesus alive. When she sees the tomb empty, she is distraught. "They have taken the Lord out of the tomb, and we don't know where they have put him!" She believes in a dead, now dishonored Jesus, not a resurrected one.

Peter and the beloved disciple run to the tomb to see if what she says is true. Peter runs into the tomb. He sees it is empty, but he still does not believe.

The beloved disciple enters the tomb, sees it empty, and believes. Believes that Jesus has been raised, even though he has yet to see the resurrected Jesus.

Mary, by contrast, still weeps over the dead and now missing Jesus. She does not recognize the resurrected Lord when she sees him, only when she hears him gently call her by name. Then she sees and believes.

She tells the disciples, "I have seen the Lord." But it seems they do not believe her. Instead, in fear they hide behind locked doors. Only when Jesus enters and they see do they all believe.

All but Thomas. He was not there to see Jesus. So a week later, Jesus appears again to all the disciples. Thomas sees, touches, believes, and confesses, "My Lord and my God."

Doubting Thomas. Doubting disciples. Doubting Mary.

Do we doubt? Do we really believe Jesus is alive? If so, why do we fear? If so, don't we hear the words of Jesus, "Peace with you!" If Jesus lives, then no power, no pain, no failure, no disappointment, nothing, not even death, can take away out peace.

We believe in the resurrected Jesus we have not seen. We believe because of the testimony of others. We believe because we have seen his love in our lives. We have heard his gentle voice call our name. We have reached out and touched him as he touched us.

And all we can do is fall on our knees and say, "My Lord and my God."

"Jesus, our Teacher, our Lord, our God. Forgive our doubts. Increase our faith. Give us your peace."

LOVE AND TESTIMONY

(John 20:30-21:25)

DAY ONE READING AND QUESTIONS:

[30]Jesus did many other miraculous signs in the presence of his disciples, which are not recorded in this book. [31]But these are written that you may believe that Jesus is the Christ, the Son of God, and that by believing you may have life in his name.

1. *Why aren't we told about more of the miraculous signs of Jesus? Wouldn't more miracle stories increase our faith? Can a book produce faith?*

2. *What does it mean to believe that Jesus is the Christ, the Son of God? What does that belief demand of us?*

3. *What kind of life is promised in the name of Jesus?*

DAY TWO READING AND QUESTIONS:

[1]Afterward Jesus appeared again to his disciples, by the Sea of Tiberias. It happened this way: [2]Simon Peter, Thomas (called

Didymus), Nathanael from Cana in Galilee, the sons of Zebedee, and two other disciples were together. ³"I'm going out to fish," Simon Peter told them, and they said, "We'll go with you." So they went out and got into the boat, but that night they caught nothing.

⁴Early in the morning, Jesus stood on the shore, but the disciples did not realize that it was Jesus.

⁵He called out to them, "Friends, haven't you any fish?"

"No," they answered.

⁶He said, "Throw your net on the right side of the boat and you will find some." When they did, they were unable to haul the net in because of the large number of fish.

⁷Then the disciple whom Jesus loved said to Peter, "It is the Lord!" As soon as Simon Peter heard him say, "It is the Lord," he wrapped his outer garment around him (for he had taken it off) and jumped into the water. ⁸The other disciples followed in the boat, towing the net full of fish, for they were not far from shore, about a hundred yards. ⁹When they landed, they saw a fire of burning coals there with fish on it, and some bread.

¹⁰Jesus said to them, "Bring some of the fish you have just caught."

¹¹Simon Peter climbed aboard and dragged the net ashore. It was full of large fish, 153, but even with so many the net was not torn. ¹²Jesus said to them, "Come and have breakfast." None of the disciples dared ask him, "Who are you?" They knew it was the Lord. ¹³Jesus came, took the bread and gave it to them, and did the same with the fish. ¹⁴This was now the third time Jesus appeared to his disciples after he was raised from the dead.

1. *Jesus has been raised from the dead, breathed the Holy Spirit on the disciples, and sent them out as the Father sent him. Why are they now going back to their old life of fishing?*

2. *Why do you think Peter jumps in the water?*

3. Why is it significant that Jesus eats with the disciples? Does this meal remind you of others he had with them?

DAY THREE READING AND QUESTIONS:

[15]When they had finished eating, Jesus said to Simon Peter, "Simon son of John, do you truly love me more than these?"

"Yes, Lord," he said, "you know that I love you."

Jesus said, "Feed my lambs."

[16]Again Jesus said, "Simon son of John, do you truly love me?"

He answered, "Yes, Lord, you know that I love you."

Jesus said, "Take care of my sheep."

[17]The third time he said to him, "Simon son of John, do you love me?"

Peter was hurt because Jesus asked him the third time, "Do you love me?" He said, "Lord, you know all things; you know that I love you."

[18]Jesus said, "Feed my sheep. I tell you the truth, when you were younger you dressed yourself and went where you wanted; but when you are old you will stretch out your hands, and someone else will dress you and lead you where you do not want to go." [19]Jesus said this to indicate the kind of death by which Peter would glorify God. Then he said to him, "Follow me!"

1. Jesus asks Peter, "Do you love me more than these"? These what? Fish? Disciples?

2. Why does Peter not claim here to love Jesus more than others? What lesson had Peter learned? How?

3. *What is the relationship between loving Jesus and feeding his sheep? What does it mean to feed his sheep?*

Day Four Reading and Questions:

[20]Peter turned and saw that the disciple whom Jesus loved was following them. (This was the one who had leaned back against Jesus at the supper and had said, "Lord, who is going to betray you?") [21]When Peter saw him, he asked, "Lord, what about him?"

[22]Jesus answered, "If I want him to remain alive until I return, what is that to you? You must follow me." [23]Because of this, the rumor spread among the brothers that this disciple would not die. But Jesus did not say that he would not die; he only said, "If I want him to remain alive until I return, what is that to you?"

[24]This is the disciple who testifies to these things and who wrote them down. We know that his testimony is true.

[25]Jesus did many other things as well. If every one of them were written down, I suppose that even the whole world would not have room for the books that would be written.

1. *Why does Peter ask about the disciple Jesus loved?*

2. *Why does Jesus reply the way he does to Peter? What does Jesus mean by "follow me"? Hasn't Peter been a follower of Jesus?*

3. *Do you think the last verse is a strange way to end the gospel? What is the point of that verse?*

Day Five Reading and Questions:

Go back and read the entire passage.

1. Even after the resurrection, do these disciples know how to follow Jesus?

2. How do we show love for Jesus? How did Peter show his love?

3. How has testimony been important in the Gospel of John?

MEDITATION ON JOHN 20:30-21:25

They begin by leaving their nets and following John the Baptist. John points them to Jesus, the Lamb of God, who takes away the sins of the world. Andrew follows Jesus, then tells his brother Simon, "We have found the Messiah." Simon comes to Jesus and is renamed Cephas (or Peter, "the rock")

Peter, Andrew and others follow Jesus to Cana, where water is turned to wine. They see Jesus give sight to a blind man, multiply loaves and fish, stop a storm in its tracks, and even raise the dead. They hear his teaching, watch him pray, and even feel their feet being washed by his hands. They follow him at a distance to his trial, witness the crucifixion, and view the empty tomb. They receive the Holy Spirit from the breath of the resurrected Jesus. They hear him say, "As the Father has sent me, so I am sending you."

Then they go back to fishing.

Why? Why aren't they out proclaiming the risen Lord? Why don't they immediately act on the mission God has given them?

Why don't we? Having believed on the risen Lord whom we have not seen, why do we fall back into our ordinary lives? Why go back to the familiar and routine?

Perhaps because we, like Peter, need to learn what it means to follow Jesus, to be disciples. Like Peter, it is easy for us to say, "We love you Lord." We say it every Sunday in church as we confess the faith and sing the hymns. What is harder is to live out our love by feeding the lambs and caring for the sheep.

It is easier to convince ourselves that we love the unseen Jesus, the one who loves and cares for us, than it is to care for needy people. People are messy. They demand our attention. They waste our time. Care giving is hard work. It can only be done by the power of the Spirit.

Perhaps, like Peter, we would rather change the subject. "How about that guy over there?" We find it easier to focus on another's walk with Jesus. But Jesus will not let us off the hook. "You must follow me", he says.

Follow to service. Follow to the cross. Follow to where we might not want to go.

But follow we must. It is the path to life.

"Lord Jesus, you appear to us in the ordinary places of life. Take us out of the ordinary, out of our concern for self. May we love you by caring for others."

The Meditative Commentary Series

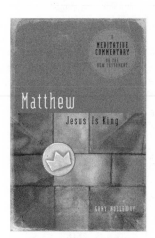
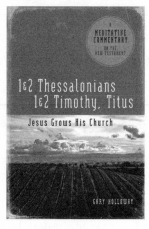
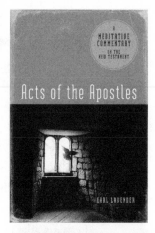
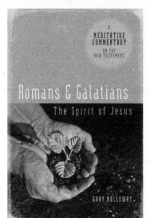

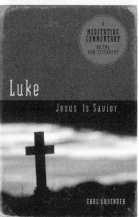